LOST
IN OUTER SPACE

by TOD OLSON

LOST IN THE PACIFIC, 1942

LOST IN OUTER SPACE

L⊘ST
IN OUTER SPACE

THE
INCREDIBLE JOURNEY
of APOLLO 13

TOD OLSON

Scholastic Inc.

Photos ©: viii bottom: Yale Joel/Getty Images; ix center right: Courtesy Sy Liebergot-Apollo EECOM
Flight Controller; ix bottom left and right: NASA/honeysucklecreek.net; 14: San Francisco Chronicle/
Polaris Images; 16: Rue des Archives/The Granger Collection; 22: Yale Joel/Getty Images; 24: Bettmann/
Getty Images; 61, 81: Photos by Eric Long, Smithsonian National Air and Space Museum (NASM 98-
16043, NASM 99-15227); 85: AP Images; 110: Bill Eppridge/Getty Images; 114: NASA/Universe Today;
121, 125: Bill Eppridge/Getty Images; 138: NASA-Apollo (digital version by Science Faction)/Getty
Images; 147: AP Images; 151, 163: NASA/Framepool; 171: Bill Eppridge/Getty Images; 175: AP Images;
185, 189: Bill Eppridge/Getty Images; 190: AP Images; 192: Leif Skoogfors/Corbis Historical/Getty
Images; 197: GSFC/Arizona State University/NASA. All other photos courtesy of NASA.

Illustrations by: cover: Shane Rebenschied; 50-51 and 65: Richard Chasemore;
65 (inset) and 90-91: Jim McMahon.

Copyright © 2017 by Tod Olson

Library of Congress Cataloging-in-Publication Data available

ISBN 978-0-545-92815-1

10 9 8 7 6 5 4 3 2 1   17 18 19 20 21

Printed in the U.S.A.   23
First edition, February 2017

Book design by Jessica Meltzer

For Finn,
who would make a pretty good stunt pilot

TABLE OF CONTENTS

CAST OF CHARACTERS

THE CREW

JIM LOVELL
Mission commander

FRED HAISE
Lunar module pilot

JACK SWIGERT
Command module pilot

THE FAMILY

THE LOVELLS

Barbara, Jay, Jeffrey, Susan, and Marilyn

MISSION CONTROL

GENE KRANZ
Lead flight
director

GLYNN LUNNEY
Black Team flight
director

JOHN AARON
Lead EECOM*

SY LIEBERGOT
White Team
EECOM*

**VANCE BRAND AND
JACK LOUSMA**
Black Team and White Team CAPCOMs†

JOE KERWIN
Gold Team CAPCOM†

*Electrical, Environmental, and Consumables Manager
†Capsule Communicator

APRIL 13, 1970

It took a lot to make Captain Jim Lovell flinch. He'd flown navy fighter jets fresh off the assembly line to see if they would hold up in midair. He'd been blasted into orbit at 17,000 miles an hour. He had been all the way to the moon and circled it ten times when no one knew for sure it was possible.

Now he was on his way to the moon again—jammed into a tiny space capsule with two other astronauts. And every time Fred Haise turned that stupid repress valve, Lovell nearly jumped out of his skin.

It was a routine procedure designed to equalize the air pressure between the two main parts of the spacecraft. But when Haise hit the valve, it jolted the ship with a hiss and a thump.

Haise was a rookie astronaut, and he couldn't resist a good practical joke. He'd already discovered that Velcro

Destination: The moon from Apollo 13.

sounded a lot like the thrusters firing outside the ship. The astronauts wore pads of the stuff on the bottom of their shoes to help anchor them in zero gravity. Every now and then, Haise would stick a Velcro pad to something and snap it in and out. That was enough to startle Jack Swigert, the third crew member.

"What's firing?" Swigert would say. "We're not supposed to be firing."

"That's my foot firing," Haise would respond.

He got just as good a reaction from the repress valve,

and he obviously enjoyed it because he turned the valve more than he needed to.

For Lovell, the mission commander, the joke had gotten old. The night sky looked beautiful from the safety of Earth, but it was a different story when you were floating in the middle of it.

Space is one of the harshest environments you can imagine. In sunlight, the spacecraft's outer shell could get as hot as an oven. In shadow it cooled to negative 100 degrees Fahrenheit. More importantly, there was almost no air pressure outside the capsule's 3-inch metal shell. If something tore a hole in the spacecraft—even one as small as a penny—air would rush from the compartment like water from a broken fish tank. Oxygen in the body would follow, probably bursting a lung on the way out. Fluid in the muscles and veins would expand into gas, causing body tissue to swell up like a balloon.

That would be it. No more mission. No chance to walk on the moon. Lovell, Haise, and Swigert would be unconscious in seconds. In two minutes, they'd be dead. The spacecraft would continue on its course, shoot around the moon, and hurtle into space like a discus at the Olympics. Only it would never come down.

When the stakes were that high, an unexpected hiss and a thump could get your imagination working fast.

And that was why the repress valve made even Jim Lovell's nerves fray.

But 55 hours into Apollo 13, humankind's third mission to the surface of the moon, everything was running smoothly. So smoothly, in fact, that it was time to host a TV show. Lovell lay back on his seat at the base of the cone-shaped command module. He stabilized himself with his feet and worked the camera with his hands. Swigert sat next to him, off camera. Haise floated at the top of the capsule, ready to host the broadcast. In yet another miracle of the space program, a video signal would leave the spacecraft and be captured by giant radio dishes on Earth: *Coming to you live—from space.*

———◆———

At the other end of that invisible relay, in Houston, Texas, Barbara Lovell waited patiently for her father's show to begin. She sat in a private room overlooking the command center, known as Mission Control, at NASA—the National Aeronautics and Space Administration. Below her, on the other side of a large plate-glass window, platoons of engineers monitored Apollo 13 around the clock. Barbara's mother, Marilyn, and her eleven-year-old sister, Susan, sat next to her. Fred Haise's wife, Mary, was there too. She was seven months pregnant with their third kid.

Astronaut Duties: A month before the launch, Barbara (left) had to pose with her family for an official NASA photograph.

Barbara was excited for her father. After all, he was going to be the fifth person ever to walk on the moon. She knew how important it was to him. But all the attention that came with being an astronaut family? That she wasn't crazy about.

At sixteen, she had already been through three of her father's space flights. Each time, reporters surrounded the family like mosquitoes—in the driveway and on their lawn. TV stations built giant broadcast towers in the street. News vans crowded onto their cul-de-sac, nosy satellite dishes poking from the roofs. Cameras and microphones prodded her every time she left the house. She had to look nice and act like the perfect kid. What to wear? Hair back or down? And the questions from the reporters were the worst:

Barbara, what did you think of the launch?

Barbara, how's your mother doing?

Barbara, what's the mood like at home?

She was shy—the kind of shy that made you hang back so much that people thought you were a snob. Most of the time she had no idea what to say to the reporters.

For now, at least, she didn't have to say a thing. Barbara sat with her family and Mary Haise and peered down at the engineers hunched over their computer screens. It was 7:24 p.m. Houston time when the cramped cockpit of her father's spacecraft flickered onto a big screen on the wall.

———◆———

Two hundred thousand miles away, Barbara's father and Fred Haise gave a tour of the spacecraft and an introduction to life in zero gravity. Haise floated around the lunar module, showing it off to the audience back at home. In two days, the LEM, as it was called, would detach from the rest of the spacecraft and take Haise and Lovell down to the surface of the moon while Swigert waited for them in orbit. On-screen, Haise tried to settle himself on a long piece of cloth stretched across the tiny compartment.

Live from Space: The engineers at Mission Control watch a wall-mounted screen as Fred Haise gives his tour of the lunar module.

"Now we can see Fred engaged in his favorite pastime," Lovell said.

"He's not in the food locker, is he?" asked Jack Lousma, the Capsule Communicator, or CAPCOM, who was on the line in Houston.

"That's his second-favorite pastime," Lovell said. "Now he's rigging his hammock for sleep on the lunar surface."

Lovell moved to a window in the lunar module and zoomed in on the moon. They were still about 40,000 miles away but closing in at 2,000 miles per hour.

7

"I can see quite distinctly some of the features with the naked eye," said Haise. "So far, though, it's still looking pretty gray, with some white spots."

It was all very casual. The crew even had nicknames for the main parts of the ship. They called the LEM *Aquarius*, after a boy from Greek mythology who supposedly carried water to the gods. The command module went by *Odyssey*. Lovell had seen a dictionary definition of the word and liked it: "a long voyage marked by many changes of fortune."

Lovell poses for the camera in the lunar module.

8

After 25 minutes of banter, Lovell made his way back into *Odyssey*. He showed off a floating tape recorder with piano jazz playing on it—a playlist for a trip to the moon.

Then he stopped in mid-sentence with a tense "Stand by . . ."

A second later, Haise's voice came across the line: "Yeah, I got 'em with the cabin repress valve again there, Jack."

"Every time he does that, our hearts jump into our mouths," Lovell said.

A few seconds later, he wished the residents of planet Earth a nice evening and signed off.

In Houston, Barbara watched the image of her father flicker out on the big screen. Then she went back to the car with her mother and sister. A public affairs officer from NASA led them out—during the flights, there was always someone with a NASA badge shadowing them.

Outside, the reporters were waiting. Thank goodness her mother was there to run interference. Marilyn Lovell recited the answers like she was reading a script: *We're very excited about the flight . . . happy for Jim . . . grateful for the brilliant people at NASA.*

Then the family headed home. It was Monday, after all; Barbara and Susan had school the next day.

While the Earth-bound Lovells drove home, the astronauts returned to the business of flying to the moon. Mission Control had a few tasks for them before they went to sleep for the night. Lousma ordered the crew to roll the spacecraft right and check the thrusters, which they did.

For the final task, Swigert located a switch that would stir the ship's oxygen and hydrogen tanks. The tanks were housed in the service module, a 25-foot-long cylinder attached to the wide base of the command module. The service module served as the ship's all-purpose engine room and essential supply cabinet. The crew had no access to it, but their lives depended on its contents. The service module contained the main engine, the electrical power supply, and enough breathable oxygen for three men to get to the moon and back. The oxygen and hydrogen were stored at extremely low temperatures that turned the gases into a kind of slush. The slush needed to be stirred from time to time in order to measure how full the tanks were.

Swigert, strapped to his seat, threw the switch to stir the tanks. Lovell drifted around the command module, attending to his duties. Haise was halfway through the hatch, returning from the lunar module.

A minute and a half into the stir, a loud metallic thud rang through the ship. Lovell flinched. Then he got mad.

He looked over at Haise, thinking the rookie must have pulled another prank with the repress valve. But Haise looked back at him with wide, frightened eyes.

"It wasn't me," he said.

Swigert looked clueless, too.

Had the spacecraft been hit by a fragment of an asteroid? At the speeds they were traveling, it wouldn't take more than a pebble to tear a hole in the ship and start the nightmare scenario in motion. But if that's what had happened, it would be over by now—and they were all still alive.

Alive, but in some kind of trouble.

Amber warning lights began to flash on the right side of the instrument panel. Something was wrong with the electrical system.

Haise and Swigert both tried to report at once.

"Okay, Houston . . ."

". . . I believe we've had a problem here."

A few seconds went by.

"This is Houston," said the CAPCOM, "say again please."

It was Lovell who answered this time. "Houston," he said, "we've had a problem."

CHAPTER 1

RACE TO OUTER SPACE

As jobs go, *astronaut* was a dangerous one. In fact, when Jim Lovell was first picked as a candidate by NASA, it seemed downright suicidal.

It was early February 1959, more than eleven years before Apollo 13 took off for the moon. Lovell was thirty years old. He had just finished test pilot training at the Pax River naval base in Maryland, where he'd graduated first in his class. His career looked good, and his family was growing. Barbara was five, his son Jay three, and little Susan just a baby.

The orders came on a Wednesday, in top secret navy jargon. Lovell was to show up in Washington, D.C., the next morning for something having to do with "Special Projects Matters." Dress in a business suit, no military markings. Tell no one where he was going, not even his wife.

The next day, Lovell found himself in a conference room with thirty-four men who looked a lot like him. They all had military buzz cuts and wore suits dug out of the backs of closets. They stood no taller than 5'11" and weighed no more than 180 pounds. Every one of them was a test pilot.

Standing before them was a man with a big, balding forehead and the look of a college professor. He was Robert Gilruth, head of the Space Task Group in a new organization called NASA. Gilruth's job was stressful enough to make anyone lose his hair. He had to put a human being in orbit around the Earth, and he had to do it before the Soviet Union did.

———◆———

At the time, the Soviet Union and the United States were as close to war as two countries could get without actually dropping bombs on each other. It was a tense global rivalry known as the Cold War. The two countries spent billions of dollars building nuclear weapons to terrify each other into submission. Sixteen months before the secret meeting Lovell attended in Washington, the Soviets had extended the "battlefield" of the Cold War—into space.

On October 4, 1957, a Soviet rocket designed to carry bombs blasted a 184-pound metal ball out of Earth's atmosphere at 17,000 miles an hour. The ball was a satellite called Sputnik 1. It was the first human-made object ever

A San Francisco newspaper announces the beginning of the Space Race.

to leave the 60-mile-thick layer of gases that supports life on Earth. This floating metal beach ball carried no explosives. It contained no spy cameras. It simply circled the globe every 98 minutes, sending out a radio signal. But to many Americans, the steady beep of that signal was the sound of time running out.

Sputnik looked like it could be the first step in a brand-new kind of war. A rocket powerful enough to blast something into space could surely carry a bomb from Moscow to Washington, D.C., in no time at all. And imagine what would happen if the Soviets put dozens of Sputniks in orbit, each one armed not with a radio transmitter, but a nuclear warhead. "It is quite possible that an aggressor nation who dominates space will dominate the world," announced the famous American air force general Jimmy Doolittle. "We just can't let that happen."

That fear was why Jim Lovell and thirty-four other test pilots sat in a conference room in the winter of 1959 disguised as civilians. They were part of a pool from which NASA would choose the first seven Americans to leave the atmosphere and fly into space.

But the way NASA planned to do it, as Gilruth described it, sounded like an invitation to their own funerals. The engineers weren't building a jet-powered plane to fly into space and back on its own power. That would take years, and no one wanted to give the Soviets that kind of lead in what everyone was now calling the Space Race. Instead, NASA planned to use a missile already developed for carrying bombs. But instead of a bomb, they would attach a tiny capsule to the top of the missile and stick a test pilot inside. Then they would blast the capsule into space from NASA's launch site on the

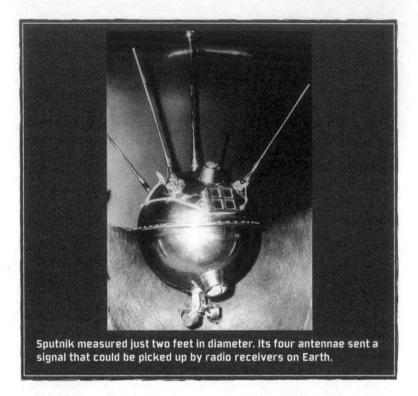

Sputnik measured just two feet in diameter. Its four antennae sent a signal that could be picked up by radio receivers on Earth.

Atlantic coast of Florida and let it parachute back down to Earth. This plan was known as Project Mercury.

Jim Lovell did not make the cut for Mercury. He watched from the sidelines while NASA got the program off the ground—or tried to. In 1960 and 1961, the missile that was supposed to carry the first astronauts into space— the Atlas—went through almost seventy tests. Nearly half of them ended in failure. And when the Atlas failed, it failed in spectacular fashion. Some of the test rockets hovered hopefully 20 feet above the ground before collapsing into massive fireballs. Others lifted straight and high and looked like a grand success. Then they wobbled, turned abruptly, and headed for Orlando or Miami or a gallery of spectators who had gathered to watch the launch. Tense seconds followed until the wayward missiles were blown to pieces by remote control.

Were they really going to put a human being on top of that thing and blast him into space?

The best-trained engineers in the country were making it up as they went along. And even if they succeeded, it wasn't entirely clear that human beings could survive in space. Scientists thought an extended stay out there might ruin an astronaut's middle ear, which would mean a life of dizziness back on Earth. Or worse, the circulatory system could refuse to pump blood without the pressure of Earth's gravity surrounding it.

———◆———

There was no question that *astronaut* was one of the most dangerous jobs you could find. Jim Lovell knew that. But it was still the job he wanted.

Lovell had been hooked on flight since high school, when he made rockets out of cardboard tubes and homemade gunpowder and watched them explode in midair just like the Atlas. And was flying in space really more dangerous than test-piloting jet fighters? When you flew

NASA had to piece together the first Mercury capsule after its Atlas rocket exploded on a test flight. Luckily, the capsule had no crew aboard.

tricky maneuvers at 400 miles an hour, all it took was one loose bolt or leaky fuel line, and a high-tech plane became a missile. When something went wrong, it was over in a second. Often, a pilot's body ended up burned beyond recognition in a heap of twisted, smoking metal. According to the navy, if a fighter pilot flew for 20 years, he stood a one in four chance of dying in a plane crash.

Sure the job would be risky. But think what you'd get in return: You'd ride the world's most powerful rockets into space. You'd see Earth the way only a handful of people in history had ever seen it. Maybe you'd even walk on the moon. The rewards had to be worth the risk.

When Lovell got a call from NASA in September 1962, he didn't hesitate. Would he become part of the second group of astronauts—the New Nine, as the newspapers would call them? Yes, he would.

He called Marilyn and told her they were moving to Houston. By that time, the Atlas had done its job. John Glenn, one of the original seven astronauts, had climbed into the tin can they called a space capsule and become the first American to circle the Earth. The Soviets had already put several Sputniks, seven dogs, dozens of mice, and two human beings into orbit. But the American space program was underway, and the Lovells were going to be a part of it.

CHAPTER 2

FIRE IN THE SPACECRAFT!

Barbara Lovell was just eight years old when her father became an astronaut. But she already knew that he risked his life for a living. Nobody in the family talked about it, but she understood. They had been living on the Pax River base, where her dad tested fighter jets for the navy. Once a month, sometimes more often, sirens sounded at the base, signaling that a plane had gone down. The men all got out their dress uniforms and went off to a funeral. Someone's father had died.

When they moved to Houston, though, Barbara learned that being part of an astronaut family came with plenty of benefits. The Lovells built a big brick house on Lazywood Lane in a development called Timber Cove. Nearly everyone there had something to do with NASA. Engineers drew spacecraft designs on cocktail napkins at parties. Barbara swam in the community pool, which was shaped like a space capsule. She rode in a Corvette leased to her dad for next to nothing by a local car dealer. And when he flew a mission, the gifts poured in. It was random stuff sometimes, like a typewriter that typed cursive. Mostly they got free jewelry and clothes. Fashion companies even sent her mom dresses; all she had to do was wear them when she went out to meet the reporters.

Jim Lovell flew into orbit for the first time in 1965, when Barbara was twelve. He went up again a year later. Both flights were part of the Gemini program, NASA's next step on the way to the ultimate goal—putting a human being on the moon. Each time her dad flew, Barbara got to bring a note to school: *Please excuse Barbara; she's going to Florida to watch her father get blasted into space.* The family would stay in a hotel and hang out on the beach or at the hotel pool. Then they'd gather to watch the liftoff, and it would dawn on her what was about to happen.

They stood on a hill overlooking the launch site. Down below was the rocket, standing tall with gaseous oxygen streaming off it like steam—all that power packed into a cylinder, and *her* father sat on top of it. That's when the sinking feeling set in—the butterflies in your stomach— waiting for something to happen. And when the engines finally lit and the fire swept the launch pad, it made the ground shake all the way up the hill, and you felt it through your whole body. "I was nervous," she told the nosy reporters once when they asked what it felt like. "I thought that the Earth was going to crack or something."

For a while, everything was fine with the flights—not just her dad's but all of them. There were no sirens, no "Breaking News" announcements on TV. Barbara's father spent two weeks in space on his first mission, longer than anyone before him.

But one night in February 1966, her mother got a call from a friend at NASA. Two astronauts, Elliot See and

Barbara (far right) watches the Apollo 8 liftoff in 1968 with Susan, Jeffrey, and their mother.

Charlie Bassett, had just crashed and burned in their T-38 trainer jet. NASA was sending someone to tell Mr. See's wife what had happened. In the meantime, they wanted Barbara's mother to go down the street and keep Mrs. See company—without announcing that her husband had just died. The Sees had two daughters who were nine and ten, only a couple of years younger than Barbara. When they found out, one of them asked her mother, "Are we still an astronaut family?"

That haunted Barbara, the thought of those kids being left without their dad.

But it wasn't as bad as when Eddie White's father burned to death inside his space capsule.

———◈———

On January 27, 1967, Barbara was at home in Houston. Her father was in Washington, D.C., at a White House dinner, shaking hands with important people.

At Cape Kennedy in Florida, astronauts Gus Grissom, Ed White, and Roger Chaffee climbed into the first Apollo command module for a test run of the liftoff procedures. The Apollo program followed Gemini, and if everything went according to plan, its missions would finally reach the moon. Its first capsule had twice been blasted into space empty, and everything had gone well. A month from now, Grissom, White, and Chaffee were going to fly the first mission with a crew aboard.

Despite the two successful launches without a crew, the astronauts weren't happy with the ship. It had logged about 20,000 different failures in testing. An important nozzle had shattered when the engine was fired. The heat shield cracked during a simulated landing in a pool. Wally Schirra, a backup pilot for the mission, told Grissom the day before the test run that the ship didn't "ring right."

"If you have any problem," Schirra said, "I'd get out."

Chaffee, White, and Grissom train in a model of the command module just a week before the test launch.

There were plenty of problems during the test, right from the start. The oxygen filling the astronauts' masks smelled like sour milk. The audio link from the capsule to the test controllers sounded terrible.

"How are we going to get to the moon if we can't talk between two or three buildings," Grissom growled into his headset.

At 6:20 p.m., the controllers put the countdown on hold while they tried to fix the audio. Eleven minutes later, they saw a figure move urgently inside the window of the capsule. A voice came crackling through the bad audio link: "Fire in the spacecraft!"

Technicians on the tower rushed across a gangway toward the spacecraft hatch. Flames shot from a vent in the capsule. A wicked orange glow flashed behind the capsule window.

In the control room, they heard Roger Chaffee's voice: "We've got a bad fire in here. We're burning up!"

On the video screen, controllers saw a pair of arms reaching past the capsule window for the bolts on the hatch. The flight surgeon, who was monitoring the astronauts' vital signs, noticed Ed White's heart rate jump.

A giant cloud of smoke erupted from the side of the capsule, and someone on the tower yelled, "She's going to blow!"

Seconds later the spacecraft gave way to the 2,500-degree fire raging inside. A seam in the vessel's aluminum shell burst with a sharp crack, and a deadly wave of heat and smoke escaped into the sky. For the astronauts in the capsule, the fiery disaster was over just 14 seconds after it had begun. Grissom, Chaffee, and White had choked to death on the fumes of the fire.

After news of the tragedy made it to the Lovell house, Barbara cried while she set the table for dinner. She didn't sob; that wasn't her way. Nor was it the way an astronaut family behaved. Generally, you didn't talk about the danger. It was just there, like a cold draft in the house. Her mom probably thought she was protecting Barbara and the other kids, but they knew—at least Barbara did. She heard the sirens at the naval base and the somber voices on TV. She could tell when her mom was anxious. Sometimes she had dreams that her dad had died. But it wasn't something they discussed.

So as Barbara circled the table, laying plates and forks and knives for herself, her mother, her two brothers, and her sister, she made sure no one noticed her crying. But she couldn't stop the tears from falling.

When she went back to school there were counselors for kids to talk to if they needed it. Then Eddie White came back for the first time. Everyone hugged him in PE class.

And somehow, life went on.

———◆———

When word of the fire reached Barbara's father at the White House dinner, he and the other astronauts holed up in a hotel room, under orders from NASA to avoid the press. They had known the Apollo 1 crew well. It was a terrible way to die, they agreed, stuck on the ground pushing buttons in a test. Everyone had to die sometime. Far better to go out in a ball of flames while steering your way back to your planet, or get stuck on the moon watching Earth rise blue and white over the horizon.

A week later, Barbara's dad traveled to Ed White's funeral at the West Point military academy in New York. He helped carry the coffin and lay it in the ground.

CHAPTER 3

LIFTOFF!

Jim Lovell got the word at 9 a.m. on April 11, 1970: Apollo 13 was a Go. That didn't mean it was time to get excited. No one would know for sure if they were launching until the final "Go/No Go" checks at T minus 5 minutes. Until then a dozen things could still go wrong.

Liftoff was scheduled for 2:13 p.m. Florida time. That was 1:13 p.m. Houston time—or, in military terms, 13:13. There had been a lot of talk in the press about the supposedly unlucky number assigned to the mission. The launch time was Mission Control's way of thumbing its nose at the doubters. A silly superstition meant nothing when you had the best science in the world on your side.

Lovell, Haise, and Swigert weren't about to get worried over a number either. But the preflight medical exam—that was enough to put them on edge. As a rule, astronauts hated doctors. All it took was one small thing out of whack and you could be scratched from the crew, watching on a TV monitor while your friends flew to the moon. In fact, it had happened just the day before to Ken Mattingly.

Mattingly was Apollo 13's scheduled command module pilot. He and Lovell and Haise had been training together for months. Then, a week before launch, they had all been exposed to German measles, and the doctors couldn't say for sure that Mattingly was immune. Swigert started training with the crew, and soon after it was announced that he would take Mattingly's place. Lovell put up a fight for his crewmate, but Mission Control didn't want their command module pilot coming down with a fever 240,000 miles from Earth. Mattingly flew off to Houston in a deep depression, and on the morning of April 11 it was Swigert getting ready to fly to the moon.

Swigert sailed through the last-minute physical along with Lovell and Haise. They sat down to the traditional prelaunch breakfast of steak, eggs, toast, and jelly. The high-protein fare was supposed to ease digestion during the long hours they would spend strapped to their seats in the spacecraft waiting for liftoff. Then, with technicians bustling around them like tailors, they wrestled themselves into their 76-pound space suits. The three men waddled out of the building and climbed into a van that drove

Geared Up: Fully suited and carrying oxygen tanks, Lovell, Swigert, and Haise leave for the launch pad.

them eight miles to the launch pad. Along the way, they passed a crowd of 7,000 people, each of them lucky enough to be admitted to Cape Kennedy for the launch. Another 100,000 or so had parked their cars in an endless line along Florida's Route 1 to watch.

None of the spectators had been allowed within three and a half miles of the launch site. The reason loomed high over the astronauts' heads as they approached the launch pad: the Saturn V rocket that was about to blast them into space.

The Saturn V was a machine of giant proportions. It stood 363 feet high—taller than the Statue of Liberty. It was 200 times more powerful than the Atlas, and it weighed as much as fifty jumbo jets when fully loaded with rocket fuel. NASA had been forced to design new vehicles just to transport it. They built a 400-foot-tall tower to hold it up. It carried enough high-explosive fuel to blow up a small city—and vaporize anyone who strayed too close at liftoff.

As Lovell rode the metal-cage elevator up the tower, he could see gaseous oxygen spewing out of the rocket's cone. It looked almost alive to him, a breathing beast with powers like nothing else on Earth. At around 320 feet, just before they reached the capsule, it suddenly sank in: *They were about to send him to the moon.*

The Beast: Cranes hoist the first stage of a Saturn V rocket for final assembly.

The crew crossed an access arm to the so-called "white room," a small, enclosed space that encompassed the hatchway to the command module. At 11:32 a.m., Captain Lovell grabbed a bar above the hatch and lumbered feet first into the spacecraft. Haise and Swigert followed. They settled into their seats, shoulder to shoulder in the base of the cone.

The basic design of the capsule, 13 feet in diameter and 11 feet high, hadn't changed since Gus Grissom, Ed White, and Roger Chaffee burned to death in it three years earlier. But Lovell and his crewmates had put the fire behind them. As they climbed into their own command module, they didn't think about all the reasons they might never climb out. After all, NASA had discovered the cause of the fire and fixed the problem. The ship that would take them to the moon had no exposed wiring in the capsule. It had a less-flammable mixture of oxygen and nitrogen in the air. Its hatch would open in seconds in an emergency.

That was pretty much enough for these men. "I think every pilot has known fear," Lovell once told a TV reporter. "But we have confidence in the equipment we're using, and that overcomes any fear we have of using it."

Besides, the equipment they were using had performed flawlessly since the fire; it had taken six Apollo crews into space. One of those flights—Apollo 8—had made Lovell,

Frank Borman, and Bill Anders the first human beings to leave Earth's gravity and orbit the moon.

That had been the high point of Lovell's career—even his life. To look down on the desolate, meteor-scarred landscape of the moon. To see Earth as a whole planet, no bigger than his thumbnail. To watch it rise over the horizon of the moon.

The only thing left for Lovell was to fly down to that desert landscape and walk on the moon. Only four human beings—in Apollo 11 and Apollo 12—had done it. And now it looked like he would get his chance, too.

———◆———

Three and a half miles away, Barbara Lovell stood looking down at the launch site from the hill reserved for the families of astronauts and other VIPs. Until the day before, she had been at home with Susan and Jeffrey. Jay was away at a military boarding school in Wisconsin. Her mom had gone to Florida to be near her father during the final days of training and had left the kids with a family friend.

This was what it meant to be an astronaut family. Barbara was used to it by now. Her father wasn't around much. He spent a lot of time training at the launch site in Florida or visiting far-flung parts of the country where pieces of the spacecraft were made. Her mother had obligations, too; there were political events and important dinners to attend. After a while, it was almost funny: When people called for her dad, she wasn't sure whether to say he was at NASA in Houston, at Cape Kennedy in Florida, or in outer space.

There were times when it felt like her dad's job took over the family. But Barbara had her own life, too. Mostly, she had her best friend, Connie Keck, whose house was a refuge when all the astronaut commotion became overwhelming. During her dad's flights, the Lovell house overflowed with NASA people coming and going, watching TV, drinking, keeping her mother company. She would escape to Connie's, where it was quiet and both parents were usually home. Connie's mom and dad drove Barbara to camp when her own parents were busy. They hosted Barbara's thirteenth birthday party just before her dad's second Gemini mission.

This time, her mom was supposed to come home and watch the launch from Houston. But Marilyn Lovell decided she didn't want to leave until Apollo 13 was safely in orbit. She called home. Barbara brought the familiar note to school. Then she made the trip to Florida with Susan and Jeffrey.

By noon on Saturday, April 11, she was watching from the hill, with the rocket breathing gas down below. This is what it was all for—the weeks with an absent dad and a distracted mom, the crazy mob of reporters, the house full of people. This is why they did it. Her father took all those trips—Houston to St. Louis to Hawaii to Florida— so he could sit on top of a steaming beast of a rocket and take the ultimate trip, off the face of the Earth.

———◆———

For two hours after they strapped into the capsule, Lovell, Haise, and Swigert followed instructions from Mission Control in Houston, where an army of engineers kept a close watch on every system in the ship. Like doctors monitoring a patient, they could tell a thousand things at a glance: fuel pressure in the rocket, electrical power in the batteries, temperature in the command module—even Jim Lovell's heart rate. For now, the astronauts were little more than robots. They set one switch after another, just as they had done dozens of times in training.

Underneath them, the Saturn V had been filling with fuel since 4 a.m.—more than 800,000 gallons of liquid oxygen, hydrogen, and kerosene. Lovell, Haise, and Swigert now sat on an explosive device as powerful as an atomic bomb. If something went wrong, they had two options. Assuming there was time, they could climb out, scramble into a gondola, and zip down a wire into a fireproof concrete bunker. Or, there was the last-ditch plan: Pull a handle to fire the escape rocket attached to the nose of the command module. Hopefully, it would blast them high enough to deploy parachutes that would bring them gently back to Earth.

As they went through all the checks, Lovell kept looking at the escape handle to make sure he knew how to use it.

By T minus 5 minutes, the Go/No Go checks were in full swing. Each engineer scanned the data from his system and made the call: safe to launch or not. Green lights began to shine on the big launch board in Houston. The spacecraft was Go. The emergency detection system: Go.

At T minus 3 minutes all systems shifted to automatic and the real countdown began.

At T minus 45 seconds, Lovell flipped a final switch to set the ship's central computer, known in NASA's private language of acronyms as the CMC. Launch control called out the final numbers: *eight . . . seven . . . six . . . ignition.* Three hundred feet below the astronauts, a set of valves opened. Vast amounts of fuel poured into five giant engines. Great tongues of flame began to leap from the nozzles. Smoke and fire billowed out across the tarmac, 15 *tons* of fuel burning every second.

Three . . . two . . . one . . . zero.

Lovell could hear the rumbling below him. He felt a jolt beneath his back.

"Liftoff!" came the voice from the Launch Control Center.

"The clock is running," Lovell responded.

From outside it was a fearsome sight—a missile the height of a 35-story building rising on a column of fire.

In the cockpit, it was simply loud. With 7 million pounds of thrust exploding through the engines below, the noise was deafening. Lovell had to tell Houston to speak up so his crew could hear.

As the rocket strained to lift more than 6 million pounds of fuel and spacecraft, Lovell felt his body pressed into his seat. He called out the increase in gravitational force as the rocket picked up speed, slicing through the atmosphere. Two and a half minutes after liftoff, they hit four Gs—four times the force of gravity on Earth. They had all been through it in the simulator, but rarely had they experienced it in flight: Your arms feel like tree trunks and your chest flattens; it takes effort to force air into your lungs.

One of the five engines on the rocket's first stage shut down two minutes early—a little worrisome, but no one in Houston seemed too concerned. And then, 30 miles high and right on target, the rest of the Stage I engines shut down. Lovell, Haise, and Swigert shot forward as the

Liftoff: Apollo 13 clears the tower on its way into Earth orbit.

force suddenly dropped to half a G. Haise felt like he was going to be blasted through the instrument panel.

The Saturn V responsible for the roller coaster ride was actually three rockets in one. Each section, or stage, was meant to serve a particular purpose. When it finished its job, it would separate from the spacecraft to lighten the load and let the next stage take over. Now, 2 minutes and 44 seconds into the flight, Stage I was done. A set of exploding bolts fired 190 feet below the crew, and a cylinder the size of a 14-story building went spinning through the air, headed eventually for a meeting with the Atlantic

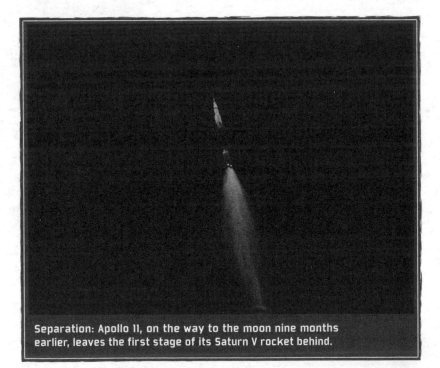

Separation: Apollo 11, on the way to the moon nine months earlier, leaves the first stage of its Saturn V rocket behind.

Ocean. From the ground it looked like an invisible knife had sliced the spacecraft in half, one section still alive and the other dying behind it.

As gravity returned to normal, Swigert and Haise started to relax. They were traveling to space for the first time. Only four dozen people out of three and a half billion had seen what they were seeing right now. Swigert caught a glimpse of the cylinder, still smoking as it tumbled toward Earth.

"Beautiful," he breathed.

"Look at that," Haise said with awe in his voice.

Lovell, who had been here three times before, was all business.

"Mode II," he called out, signaling the switch to the Stage II engines.

"Look at the horizon out there," Haise said.

Outside the window was an awesome sight. From the ground you had to take it for granted that the Earth was round. Now, 50 miles high and climbing, Haise could actually see the curve in the globe. The endless hours he'd spent in a simulator, the tests, the pictures, and the studying—none of it had really prepared him for this.

"13, Houston," came the CAPCOM's voice, flat and reassuring. "Guidance is good, and the CMC is GO."

They were on their way to Earth orbit—first stop on the way to the moon.

CHAPTER 4

ZERO G

Thirteen minutes into the flight, Apollo 13 settled into orbit around the Earth.

"Everything is looking good," the CAPCOM reported.

"Roger, Houston," Lovell said. "And it looks good to be up here again."

The engine failure on the first stage had the crew worried on their way into orbit. After it quit early, they had to burn the second stage for longer than expected to make up for it. But the engineers in Houston insisted they had plenty of fuel left to get the spacecraft to the moon. Lovell figured that every mission had its glitch—one thing that doesn't go according to plan. Hopefully, they had gotten theirs out of the way, and now they were home free.

The astronauts unstrapped from their seats, and Haise and Swigert got their first taste of real zero gravity.

"Jack, be careful in your movements," Lovell warned, the veteran watching out for the rookie.

Lovell had spent more than 500 hours floating in space. Haise and Swigert had only their training time underwater in SCUBA gear—plus a few flights in the "Vomit Comet." That's what they called the KC-135 jet plane that NASA used to simulate zero gravity. The trainees sat in the cargo hold, unstrapped but hooked to a nest of medical sensors. The plane rocketed skyward, accelerating all the way. When it hit about 40,000 feet and 500 miles per hour, with 2Gs of force pushing the astronauts into the floor, the pilot cut the engine and started to nose over in a wide arc. The G forces vanished, and there they were, floating in the back of the plane. They'd practice flipping switches on a control panel just like the one in the spacecraft. All the while the sensors recorded their pulse and their blood pressure and whatever else the doctors wanted to know.

It was a wild ride, but it was over before it started. The entire experience lasted 30 seconds if the pilot was good. That was the best they could do down on Earth, where the laws of nature held you fast to the planet. With a little flying skill—and a lot of jet fuel—you could cheat gravity for a fleeting moment. But you couldn't escape it.

Now they'd truly broken free, and what a feeling it was. Bill Anders, who had flown to the moon with

Astronauts from the Mercury program train for zero G in the cargo hold of a "Vomit Comet."

Lovell in Apollo 8, said that zero G turned you into a big jellyfish—and tests had shown that was about right. Before the Mercury flights the scientists had strapped a test subject to a beach chair and floated him in a tank of warm water for a week. When they hauled him out his muscles had gone soft, his blood pressure had dropped, and his bones already showed signs of deterioration.

But for Lovell, Haise, and Swigert, there wasn't time to float around like jellyfish. There were helmets to stow, cameras to set up, systems to check—and none of it was easy in zero G. Your head felt like an over-full water balloon because the blood that normally got pulled toward your feet by gravity stayed in your brain. You also had to think ahead just to move around. Push off from one side of the capsule a little too hard and you bounced off the other side like a Ping-Pong ball with nothing to slow you down. It could be fun, but too much of it and you began to understand how the KC-135 got its nickname.

One day into the flight, Haise washed down a few bacon cubes with some juice and promptly threw it all up. There were bags designed for exactly this purpose, and he managed to grab one in time. It was a happy moment in the small, poorly ventilated spacecraft. Stray liquid in zero G tended to float in large, stinking globules until it could be captured on a rag.

Aside from a little queasiness, the start of the mission couldn't have gone more smoothly. At 2 hours 35 minutes in, it was time to leave the Earth behind. Swigert fired the last stage of the Saturn rocket. The spacecraft accelerated toward 25,000 miles an hour, straining against the gravity that held it in orbit. In five minutes, the third stage had done its job. It pushed Apollo 13 out of orbit and propelled it toward the moon at a speed almost impossible to imagine by earthbound standards: from Boston to

Washington, D.C., in a minute; from start to finish in a 10K race in less than a second.

The moon would require a more leisurely three-day trip. It was, after all, 240,000 miles away.

Inside the spacecraft, the crew barely felt like they were moving at all. Out the windows there were no trees or fences or telephone poles flying past—just the blackness of space. Lovell, Haise, and Swigert had only two signs that they were leaving their planet in the dust. For one thing, radio communication came with a delay now. More impressively, the Earth was transforming slowly from a vast carpet of land and water below them into a distinct blue-and-white orb glowing in the sky. Four hours into the flight and 10,000 miles out, they could see the entire globe. After seven hours, Haise snapped a series of pictures. The Earth was half illuminated, half in shadow. They'd seen the moon like that hundreds of times, but never their own planet. From down there, the Earth was the *whole* world, no question about it. From up here, it looked vibrant and alive, bigger and brighter than anything else. But it was only *one* world out of many.

———◆———

Until they reached lunar orbit, the crew would be busy with housekeeping duties. Haise, as pilot of the lunar

Earth from Apollo 13, 35,000 miles away.

module, wouldn't have much to do until they powered up his part of the ship at around 55 hours. Two days later—according to the flight plan—he would detach the LEM from the rest of the spacecraft and help Lovell pilot it 60 miles down to the surface of the moon.

Swigert, the command module pilot, would stay in lunar orbit in the CSM—the combined command and service module—until Lovell and Haise finished their stay on the moon. When the LEM blasted back into orbit, Swigert would manuever the CSM to dock with it. After Lovell and Haise climbed back aboard, they would jettison the LEM, letting it drift alone in lunar orbit until it eventually crashed into the moon. Swigert would then help Lovell pilot the rest of the ship home.

Just before they entered Earth orbit, they would jettison the service module, leaving the crew with nothing but the tiny cone of the command module. In it they would enter Earth's atmosphere for the first time in eight days, and three big, billowing parachutes would lower them to an easy splashdown in the Atlantic Ocean.

That was their whole mission in a nutshell. It sounded simple when you laid it out like that—if you didn't mention the hundreds of engineers doing brilliant work for a decade, the thousands of intensely precise mathematical calculations, or the billions of dollars in state-of-the-art equipment needed to get them to the moon and back.

The astronauts controlled that equipment from the console in front of Swigert's seat. There were nine panels with more than 250 gauges monitoring everything from cabin pressure to oxygen levels to electrical power supply. The crew also had 500 buttons, knobs, switches, and dials at their fingertips. Most of the controls were protected by U-shaped metal brackets to make sure a stray hand or elbow didn't reboot the computer or depressurize the spacecraft.

It looked complicated, and it was. But piloting a spacecraft didn't take the kind of hands-on, split-second decision making that it took to pilot a jet plane. In Apollo 13, Lovell, Haise, and Swigert had to check their course against the position of the stars. They had to burn the main engine to make a few course corrections. They fired an array of small thrusters to control the spacecraft's alignment in space. Aside from that they checked pressure gauges, monitored electrical readouts, and adjusted communications antennae. But mostly, the computer flew the ship.

At around 23 hours, after their first 10-hour rest period, Lovell told Houston they'd had a "fairly good night's sleep."

THE SHIP

LUNAR MODULE

Crew compartment
House the astronauts while
they explore the lunar
surface

Descent engine
Slow down the LEM as it
lands on the moon

Fuel tanks
Power the LEM
descent engine

Docking tunnel
Connect the CM to
the LEM

Hydrogen tanks
Provide propellent for the thrusters and fuel to generate electricity

SERVICE MODULE

Fuel tanks
Power the main engine

Main engine nozzle
Make major course corrections

Antenna
Send and receive communications to and from Earth

Oxygen tanks
Provide gas for breathing and fuel to generate electricity

Thrusters
Make minor adjustments to the spacecraft's position in space

Instrument panel
House main controls for the spacecraft

Fuel cells
Combine oxygen and hydrogen to generate electricity for the spacecraft

COMMAND MODULE

"Okay. Real fine," said Joe Kerwin, the CAPCOM on duty. "About the only major thing on the spacecraft is that it's been getting farther away."

Kerwin went on to report the news: The Houston Astros had won; an earthquake had hit the Philippines; the Beatles had broken up.

Swigert admitted he had forgotten to file his income tax return, and Houston assured him they would get him an extension.

"Jack, the preliminary indications are that you can get a 60-day extension on your income tax if you're out of the country," the CAPCOM said.

"That's good news," said Swigert. "I guess I qualify."

At one point, Lovell pointed the TV camera out the window at a shower of silvery, frozen droplets glistening in the sky.

"Think you could guess what that might be?" Haise asked, with a little mischief in his voice.

Swigert explained that they had just executed a waste-water dump. Apollo 13 was headed for the moon, escorted by a cloud of frozen urine.

The banter was so casual it sounded like college buddies together for a reunion. Only the bursts of static and high-pitched beeps hinted that half the party was on its way to the moon.

That, and the fact that most of the conversation sounded like this:

Lovell: "We've retrieved Jack's dosimeter, and it's reading 02022."

Kerwin: "Okay. We copy 02022 on the dosimeter, Jim."

Lovell: "That's affirm."

Kerwin: "13, Houston. At your convenience, we'd like the LEM/CM Delta-P reading."

Lovell: "That reading is 0.65 psi."

Kerwin: "Copy 0.65, Thank you."

After the second rest period, more than 46 hours into the flight, Lovell reported that Haise, his lunar module pilot, or LMP, had lived up to his reputation as an expert at leisure activities: "LMP had a solid nine hours of sleep; I couldn't wake him up this morning."

"Spacecraft is in real good shape as far as we're concerned," Kerwin reported from Houston. "We're bored to tears down here."

In a few hours, Lovell and Haise would give their TV tour of the spacecraft. Barbara and her family would watch from the space center, then go home to bed. Several minutes later, boredom would be the last thing Kerwin, the engineers, or the astronauts had to worry about.

CHAPTER 5

WE'VE HAD A PROBLEM

Houston, we've had a problem."

Lovell's words came at 9:07 p.m. Houston time, clipped and matter-of-fact. The engineers in Mission Control had to read between the lines to hear the tension in his voice, but the flight surgeon did not. He sat just to the left of the CAPCOM in front of a long row of monitors, staring at the readout from the astronauts' medical sensors. In a matter of seconds, three heart rates jumped from 70 beats per minute to more than 130.

And this time, it wasn't the repress valve.

When that dull metallic bang rocked the ship nearly 56 hours into the mission, Haise was still in the tunnel, coming back from the lunar module after the TV broadcast. He could actually see a shock wave ripple through the metal walls around him. Two seconds later, the high-pitched master alarm squealed in his headset.

Lovell heard it too, an ear-splitting sound that was enough to make anyone's heart race. He looked at the instrument panel and saw an array of lights that should not have been on—yellow, amber, red. One of them stood out.

"We've had a main bus B undervolt," he announced abruptly.

One of two buses in the command module—the panels that distribute electricity from the fuel cells to the equipment—looked like it had gone dead.

"Okay, stand by, 13; we're looking at it," came the reply from Houston.

Haise floated down from the tunnel and tried to make sense of the gauges on the instrumentation panel. The needle measuring oxygen levels in one of their two main tanks dipped to 20 percent for a moment. Then it bounced back up over the "full" mark. The power in main bus B came back. Then it dropped again. Maybe—just maybe— it was only the gauges that were going haywire.

———◦———

In the windowless control room in Houston, Gene Kranz's headset was squawking. He was the flight director on duty at the time, in charge of a team of flight controllers, the safety of three astronauts, and the success of a $400 million

Gene Kranz works the flight director's console during a later Apollo mission.

mission. He stood on the third tier in an amphitheater-like setup, looking down on his two rows of controllers. They called it the "Trench" down there—the place where the real work gets done. Each controller was responsible for a system on board the spacecraft: guidance and navigation; flight path; reentry; communications; electricity, air, and water, and so on. They sat at computer monitors with a dizzying array of numbers scrolling past.

Right now the numbers weren't making sense, and the controllers wanted Kranz to know about it: The computer on board the ship had shut down and restarted; the radio signal had switched antennas abruptly.

Then Sy Liebergot's voice came through the headset from the console just below Kranz's: "We may have had an instrumentation problem, Flight."

Liebergot was the EECOM on duty—the Electrical, Environmental, and Consumables Manager. He was in charge of pretty much everything that kept the spacecraft running and the astronauts alive. And he couldn't believe what he was seeing on his screen. It looked like he had lost two out of Apollo 13's three fuel cells, one of two main buses, and one of two oxygen tanks. The second oxygen tank seemed to be losing ground fast. If that much of the spaceship had failed, the crew would be dead. It had to be the gauges that were going haywire, he told himself. It had to be an instrumentation problem.

A minute passed, then two, and Kranz's voice came through again, edgy this time, like he was ready for some answers. "EECOM, it looks like a lot of instrumentation problems here."

"That's affirm . . . ," Liebergot answered.

What else could he say? Three minutes into the problem and he hadn't come up with anything solid. Like all the controllers, he had spent endless hours training for just this kind of thing. Hundreds of times, they had sat at their consoles with the astronauts inside a model of the spacecraft in another room. The directors programmed problems into the system, and the controllers had to react. *Read the numbers. Diagnose the problem. Decide what to do.* They had done it over and over again until he couldn't imagine a situation they hadn't prepared for. When the time came and the situation was real, you fell back on your training and you worked the problem.

And yet, in all the hundreds of simulations, he had never seen a problem like this.

"Well"—it was Kranz again, pressing him—"let's get some recommendations here, Sy, if you got any better ideas."

On Liebergot's left, he could hear the CAPCOM, Jack Lousma, stalling for time while the crew ran down the list of problems they saw.

Lovell reported half the thrusters were out.

"Roger," said Lousma.

"We got a main bus A undervolt now, too, showing," said Haise.

"Main A undervolt," said Lousma.

Half the spacecraft seemed to be dying, and they had nothing to tell the astronauts.

Finally, Liebergot suggested the crew reset the connections between the fuel cells and the buses. Maybe the jolt in the spacecraft had jarred them loose.

"Okay, Houston," Haise reported. "I tried to reset and fuel cell 1 and 3 are both showing zip on the flows."

"We copy," Lousma said. Then he switched off the air-to-ground communications loop so the astronauts couldn't hear him.

"Are there any kind of leads we can give them?" he asked. "Are we looking at instrumentation or have we got a real problem or what?"

Gone was the easy banter that had filled the airwaves for two-and-a-half days. Now everyone needed answers, and they needed them fast. Lousma, like all CAPCOMs, was a fellow astronaut; he needed something to tell the crew. Kranz, as flight director, had final responsibility for the whole operation; he needed something to tell Lousma.

All their questions had landed in Liebergot's lap, and he didn't have the answers. Most problems were diagnosed in a matter of minutes; that's how well-trained they were. But this one didn't make sense. Too many things were going wrong at once.

For two minutes, they said nothing at all to the crew, while Kranz kept at Liebergot over the headset. He wanted to know what they had on the spacecraft that was still working fine. And he wanted to make sure that as they fumbled around for solutions they didn't ruin what was working.

Finally, Swigert's voice came through: "Okay, Houston. Are you still reading 13?"

"That's affirmative," said Lousma. "We're trying to come up with some good ideas for you."

———◆———

In the spacecraft, Lovell had at least one idea of his own. He wanted to get the hatch to the LEM closed fast. He knew the shell of the lunar module hadn't been breached; they'd all be dead if it had. But if the problem came from that direction, he wanted to make sure it stayed there. He and Swigert drifted up to wrestle with the hatch.

Haise sat in his seat on the right side of the capsule and tried to help Houston troubleshoot the problem. The suggestions weren't exactly flying through his headset. Meanwhile, the readouts on the fuel cells stared at him from the instrument panel: fuel cell 1, completely dead; fuel cell 3, completely dead.

Right in front of him, hanging on the panel, was a card listing the mission rules. He didn't even need to look. He knew they had to have three functioning fuel cells to go into lunar orbit. Haise felt his heart sink. Unless it really was just the instruments going haywire, he would not be walking on the moon.

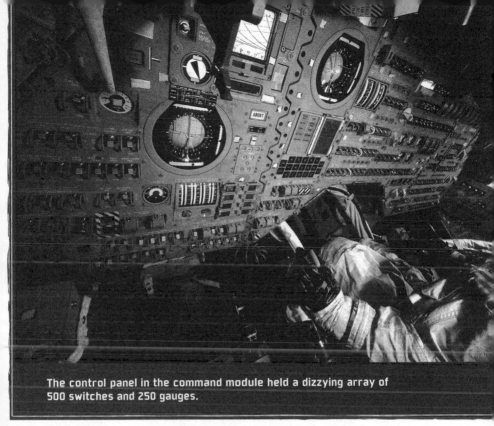

The control panel in the command module held a dizzying array of 500 switches and 250 gauges.

What had not occurred to him yet was the thought that he might never walk on Earth again.

By this time, 14 minutes into the problem, Lovell was back in front of the instrument panel. He reminded Houston that oxygen tank 2 was reading completely empty. Then, for the first time since the bang, he glanced out the window on the left side of the cockpit. What he saw raised a deep, queasy feeling in the pit of his stomach—and it had nothing to do with zero gravity. A stream of white gas drifted ominously away from the spacecraft. He couldn't see the source of the gas, but it had to be escaping from the service module.

"It looks to me, looking out the hatch, that we are venting something," he reported to Houston. "We are venting something out into the—into space."

CHAPTER 6

A DYING SHIP

Lovell's report was still scratching through the air-ground loop when Kranz repeated the words to no one in particular.

"Crew thinks they are *venting* something."

"Roger, we copy your venting," Lousma said to the crew.

"It's a gas of some sort," Lovell reported.

Five seconds ticked by, then ten, while the news sunk in: Broken gauges did not vent gas into space. What they had was a *real* problem, not an instrumentation problem. And *real* problems put men—not just missions—in danger.

Finally, Kranz said, "Okay, let's everybody think of the kind of things we'd be venting."

"Let me look at the system, Flight, as far as the venting is concerned," Liebergot said.

"I assume you've called in your backup EECOM, see if we can get more brain power in here," Kranz said.

"We got one in here," Liebergot replied abruptly.

Every console in the control room had handles on either side of the monitors, as though the controllers might someday need to hang on for dear life. Liebergot started using them. The room was full of people, his headset full of chatter—and he had never felt so alone in his life.

Fall back on the training and work the problem.

Liebergot's head was full of questions: What exactly was venting? Where was it venting from? What was still good on the spacecraft, and how could they salvage it? On his desk he had a diagram of the spacecraft's electrical system. Tanks in the service module fed hydrogen and oxygen into the fuel cells. When the two gases combined under pressure, the chemical reaction produced both electricity and water. The fuel cells then fed the electrical power into the buses, which distributed it to all the equipment on board the command module.

So far, he had reports of some kind of jolt; he had an oxygen tank reading zero; and he had some kind of gas venting into space. It didn't take much to figure out that the gas was probably oxygen. But NASA didn't launch a spacecraft without backup systems and then backups for the backups. They had two oxygen tanks and three

SERVICE MODULE

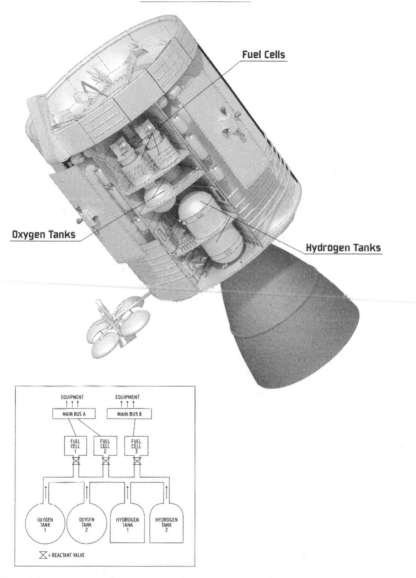

Fuel Cells

Oxygen Tanks

Hydrogen Tanks

EQUIPMENT
↑ ↑ ↑
MAIN BUS A

EQUIPMENT
↑ ↑ ↑
MAIN BUS B

FUEL
CELL
1

FUEL
CELL
2

FUEL
CELL
3

OXYGEN
TANK
1

OXYGEN
TANK
2

HYDROGEN
TANK
1

HYDROGEN
TANK
2

☒ = REACTANT VALVE

Liebergot had a diagram like the one above (inset) showing how oxygen and hydrogen combined in the fuel cells to produce electricity for the spacecraft.

fuel cells so that one could fail and the mission would barely miss a beat. Why, then, had they lost two out of three fuel cells? And why was the second oxygen tank failing too?

What he did know is that they seemed to be losing the command module, and if they kept going like this, they'd soon be out of power.

"Okay EECOM, I'm comin' back to you." It was Kranz, looking for answers again.

"Flight," Liebergot said, "I think the best thing we can do is start a powerdown."

———◆———

On board the spacecraft, the needle on the gauge for oxygen tank 1 was moving like the hand of a ticking clock. It didn't drop like a gas gauge in a car, too slowly to notice. Lovell could actually *see* it move—the life's blood of the command module slipping away.

There had never been much question in his mind that they had a *real* problem. In Houston, all they had were numbers on a screen. In the spacecraft they *felt* the jolt of that first bang. They *heard* the squeal of the master alarm. They *saw* the warning lights flash. Now they could see the gas escaping into the void. And if they looked

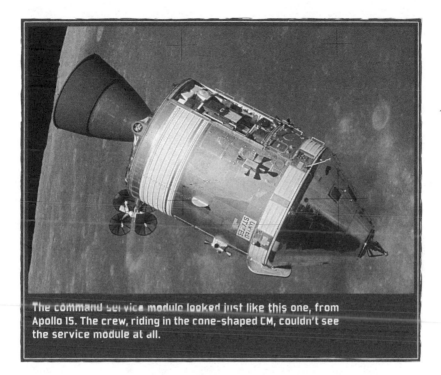

The command service module looked just like this one, from Apollo 15. The crew, riding in the cone-shaped CM, couldn't see the service module at all.

closely, they could pick out tiny fragments of metal—no more than four inches long—floating along with them toward the moon. Whatever happened back there in the service module had blasted a piece of their spacecraft into bits.

To make matters worse, the ship was lurching around in space like a balloon with a hole in it. Normally, the computerized guidance system fired the thrusters automatically to keep the ship rotating slowly like a piece of meat on a spit. That kept the sun from overcooking one side of the spaceship and freezing the other side. Now the gas escaping from the service module acted like an unauthorized thruster, pushing the ship out of alignment. The computer was firing the thrusters right and left to correct for it.

But despite all the evidence staring them in the face, Lovell, Swigert, and Haise were blind. They didn't have the data Houston had. They didn't have dozens of engineers examining the numbers.

Houston had all of that—and they still had no answers. Right now, they had Lovell's crew going through a checklist, flipping switches to turn off unnecessary instruments, lights, and heaters. That was all fine; at least it would give them more time with the power they had left. But it was little more than a Band-Aid over a bullet wound. It wasn't a cure.

"Okay, 13." It was Lousma's voice through the air-ground loop, promising information—at some point in the future. "We've got lots and lots of people working on this; we'll give you some dope as soon as we have it, and you'll be the first one to know."

"Oh, thank you," said Lovell. He couldn't keep the sarcasm from slipping into his voice.

———◆———

Liebergot had no hard information. All he had was an oxygen supply that was dwindling at a rate of 2 pounds per square inch, or psi, every minute. The command module had lost more than three-quarters of its oxygen and would be dead in two hours, maybe less. Liebergot had the crew fire up the heaters in the tank to try to bring the pressure up. It was just a stab in the dark, not an answer. And when the crew switched on the heaters, the oxygen needle kept moving in the same direction: down.

Little by little, Liebergot was being pushed toward a conclusion—and a last-ditch solution. The main systems that kept the command module running—the fuel cells and the oxygen tanks—were dying. That was only too clear from the jumble of bad numbers on Liebergot's screen. But two seats to his right sat the TELMU, the controller in charge of all the systems on the lunar module—and his screen looked fine. The LEM had its own completely independent supply of oxygen and power, designed to take Lovell and Haise on a two-day excursion to the surface of the moon. As far as anyone could tell, it had not been damaged. Maybe, if they worked it just right, the LEM could keep the astronauts alive and the spacecraft running long enough to get them back to Earth.

The LEM as lifeboat. It was an idea they had worked on in simulations before. There were plenty of reasons why it was a long shot, but at this point, it was all they had.

Liebergot clicked onto the flight director's loop. "Flight, EECOM. The pressure in O_2 tank 1 is all the way down to 297. We better think about getting in the LEM."

Kranz pressed Liebergot to find a way to save the oxygen tank. But he knew they were running out of options.

"TELMU from Flight," he said into his headset. "I want you to get some guys figuring out minimum power in the LEM to sustain life."

———◆———

More than 200,000 miles away, Lovell, Haise, and Swigert were coming to the same conclusion as Houston. They could feel the command module dying around them. Half the instruments were down to save power. The mechanical hum that normally filled the cabin had faded noticeably. The cabin lights were low. Without the instruments and the lights to warm the air, the temperature had dropped below 60 degrees Fahrenheit.

They could take refuge in the LEM, they knew that. They might even be able to make its life support systems last all the way back to Earth orbit. But the command module was their only ticket back to the surface of their planet. When they tried to penetrate the dense gases of Earth's atmosphere at 25,000 miles per hour, friction would engulf the ship in a 5,000-degree fireball. Only the command module had a heat shield that could keep them from roasting alive.

Houston was already thinking along the same lines. The command module had its own batteries and a small oxygen tank to get it back into the atmosphere after the crew jettisoned the service module. Right now the crew was using those batteries to shore up the failing fuel cells. The order came from Lousma to disconnect the batteries and save them for reentry.

Houston wanted to make one last-ditch effort to save the oxygen tank in the service module. It was still possible that the tank was fine, and the gas was leaking through the bad fuel cells. If they closed the reactant valves—the valves that let oxygen through to the cells—maybe the leak would stop. The only problem was, when you closed the reactant valves you couldn't reopen them. The fuel cell was gone for good. And that meant, once and for all, that the lunar mission was over. They had known it for a while in the back of their minds, but now there was no escaping it: They'd reached the point of no return.

"Okay, 13, this is Houston," came Lousma's voice, crackling through the air-ground loop. "It appears to us that we're losing O_2 flow through fuel cell 3. So, we want you to close the reac valve on fuel cell 3."

"Did I hear you right?" Haise said.

"That's affirmative. Close the reac valve on fuel cell 3."

Haise checked again: "Okay . . . do you want me to go through that whole smash for fuel cell shutdown? Is that correct?"

It was. And as Haise started flipping switches, both he and Lovell knew that they had probably lost the only chance they would ever have to walk on the moon.

But after they shut down fuel cell 3, and then fuel cell 1, Swigert looked at the oxygen gauge again. It read just over 200 psi and still dropping. The command module would go dark in less than 30 minutes.

"Does it look like it's still going down?" Swigert asked, hoping maybe things looked better in Houston than they did in the command module.

"It's slowly going to zero," Lousma said, "and we're starting to think about the LEM lifeboat."

"Yes," Swigert answered. "That's what we're thinking too."

CHAPTER 7
LIFEBOAT

J ust an hour before NASA began to give up on the Apollo 13 command module, Barbara Lovell had been watching her father show off his spacecraft on the monitors at the space center. His voice had sounded easy and relaxed—like he was out for a Sunday drive in his Corvette: *Aren't the seats comfortable? See how easy it shifts. And oh, by the way, check out the Earth outside the window.*

Barbara's mother definitely thought her dad seemed fine. When they got home, she told the family friend who had been watching Jeffrey, "They look like they're having fun up there."

It had taken the family 15 minutes to drive from NASA to Timber Cove. Jeffrey was asleep. A protocol officer from NASA was there, reading a magazine on the couch. Barbara could never figure out why they needed the extra attention. It was like having the Secret Service watching over you.

Barbara went upstairs and got ready for bed. Her father was going to walk on the moon, and she was happy for him. But she also knew what it meant down here on Earth: people in the house all the time, reporters to deal with, extra duties with Jeffrey. She had spent a lot of time watching her little brother while her mom went to NASA dinners and visited her dad at the Cape. It was fine, really; she loved Jeffrey. But he had called her "Mama" for the longest time after he learned to talk.

It was around 10 p.m. when Barbara heard a commotion downstairs. She went out to the landing and listened through the railing. The phone rang a few times. The TV news was on. The door opened and closed. Pete Conrad, another astronaut, and his wife were down there talking to her mother. Some other friends were there too.

Something was wrong; guests normally didn't come over this late. Barbara couldn't tell what it was, but she could hear the stress in people's voices. She didn't want to go downstairs where she'd have to ask and answer questions. Whatever it was, it couldn't be too bad, she thought. NASA would figure it out. She went back to her room and got in bed. A short while later, a friend of her mother's came up and whispered her name. Barbara pretended she was asleep.

———◆———

At Mission Control, there was no sleep in sight for Gene Kranz's White Team. The controllers worked in four shifts, with each team identified by a color. At 10:20 p.m., an hour and 10 minutes after the accident, the White Team shift was over. But no one was going home. Kranz handed over his headset to Glynn Lunney, flight director of the Black Team. He told his flight controllers to head downstairs to the airless conference rooms on the 2nd floor. There, they would join dozens of assistant controllers who were already working the problem. They would dig back into the second-by-second logs of all the systems and try to figure out what had gone wrong. Eight and a half minutes had passed between the end of the TV broadcast and the bang. Somewhere in the stream of numbers, there had to be a clue.

With a few dozen of the best engineering minds in the country, they'd uncover the cause of the problem. In the meantime, they'd figure out how to get the ship home with three healthy astronauts aboard.

Sy Liebergot pried himself loose from the handles

on his console and gave up his seat to the Black Team EECOM.

Liebergot had never been so relieved in his life.

———◆———

As the White Team cleared out, Lunney took over the flight director's headset and started grilling his flight controllers. Kranz had been edgy, but also confident and reassuring. Now tension crackled through the loop. Once, twice, three, four times Lunney went around the room asking if the controllers had done everything possible to save oxygen tank 1. He checked with the EECOM to make sure it wasn't just the gauges. He even went back to tank 2, which had been reading zero since 9 p.m. Wasn't there something they could do to bring it back?

An hour and a half had passed since the crisis, and the flight director was still hoping the problem wasn't real.

"Geez, it's really going down," he said out loud over the loop, watching the contents of tank 1 leak away.

At 10:42, they were down to 18 minutes' worth of oxygen. That meant 18 minutes of power, 18 minutes until the command module went dark, 18 minutes to power up the LEM and get it ready to keep three men alive and somehow fly the entire spaceship back to Earth.

Now the chatter on the flight director's loop was constant. Could they get the LEM powered up before they ran out of power in the command module? What could they shut down to give them more time? How much of the command module's oxygen and battery power could they use and still have enough left for reentry?

Lunney could feel the stress building as they started to shut down the command module. They would have to bring it to life again to get the crew back into Earth's atmosphere. But no one had ever tried to start up a command module in the middle of space. Suppose the instruments

Glynn Lunney works the flight director's console while a group of controllers gathers around him.

were too cold. Suppose the thrusters wouldn't fire or the computer wouldn't start. They could potentially work around the clock for days to get the crew back to Earth orbit, only to leave them stranded there forever, like a lifeless TV satellite.

"Look, I'm worried about shutting this thing down so that it's safe when we want to repower from the reentry batteries," Lunney said into the loop.

He asked his controllers if they could keep the heaters on in the guidance system—essentially the spacecraft's GPS. Without the guidance system, there would be no way to navigate their way back into Earth's atmosphere.

"How many amps do they take?" he asked.

"Ten."

"Oh, ten amps?!" The answer hit Lunney hard. "I'm lookin' at 80 hours!"

Lunney did some quick calculations. Just leaving that heater on would kill the reentry batteries in 12 hours. Without the big fuel cells in the service module, the command module was crippled. They had no choice but to power all the way down. They would have to roll the dice and take their chances.

In the spacecraft, it was obvious the command module was dying fast. Oxygen tank 1 read about 100 psi, barely enough pressure left to push the gas into the fuel cell—much less into the air that Lovell, Haise, and Swigert had to breathe. Lovell knew exactly what Lunney knew: They would have to fire up the command module's reentry batteries again. But every bit of power they used now meant that much less left to get them back into Earth's atmosphere when the time came.

If the time came.

That thought had crossed Lovell's mind when he first saw the gas from his ship venting into space. But right now, who had time to worry about whether they were going to live or die? And what good would it do them anyway? Anyone who wasted time wondering whether he'd still be alive tomorrow was not working the problem.

Haise got out his binder full of procedures and started scrawling instructions from Lousma: "LEM power switch, reset and release. In the LEM, on panel 11 and panel 16, translunar bus tie. Both circuit breakers close . . ." It went on like that for more than a minute. Haise read the instructions back carefully and then started throwing switches.

The LEM began to spring to life: cabin lights, lamps

on the instrument panel, the low hum of machinery. Lovell and Haise floated through the tunnel and got to work. Swigert stayed in the command module, using precious power from one of their reentry batteries to keep his part of the ship running while they got the LEM powered up.

What followed was a crazy flurry of commands from the ground and responses from space. Normally, space flight was so structured, a perfect symphony with every movement planned and timed and conducted with precision from the ground. Right now, it was all improvisation. Houston invented new procedures in hurried conversations. Orders flashed across 210,000 miles of space. The crew scrawled notes in the margins of their binders or crossed out steps on preset lists of procedures. They moved as fast as they dared, the command module sucking power from the reentry batteries with every passing second. At one point, Lousma told Swigert to power down the thrusters on the command module before the thrusters on the LEM were up. For a few minutes the entire spacecraft drifted in space without a computer or pilot in control.

Finally, as they approached midnight Houston time, the LEM was up and ready to go. Nearly three hours had passed since the accident. They had run through a quarter of the power from the reentry batteries, but that concern was now at the bottom of the list.

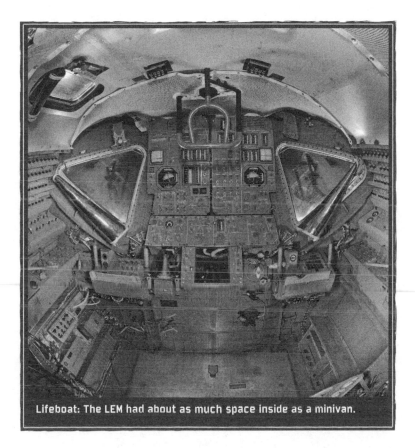
Lifeboat: The LEM had about as much space inside as a minivan.

Standing shoulder to shoulder in the LEM, Lovell and Haise were grateful to have a home. But could it really get them back to Earth? The LEM was a great ship—for a 60-mile, 45-hour trip to the lunar surface and back. That's what it was built for, and no more. Every extra pound on the LEM required three extra pounds of fuel, so the designers had saved weight wherever they could. The aluminum shell was no thicker than four layers of tinfoil. Rumor had it that workmen had dented it by dropping screwdrivers on the floor. The flimsy thing didn't even have seats. And worse, it was only stocked with oxygen, electricity, and water to support two astronauts for two days. On the current flight plan, it would take *four* days to get *three* men back to Earth.

The third of those men—Jack Swigert—was still in his darkened command module. At 11:50 p.m. Houston time, he finished powering down. He closed the valves on fuel cell 2, which had finally died along with the last oxygen tank.

"Odyssey is completely powered down, according to the procedure that you read to Jack," Lovell announced to Houston.

"Roger, we copy," said Lousma. "That's where we want to be, Jim."

Swigert turned the lights out and lingered for a while. This was his vehicle. He had spent hundreds of hours in its grounded twin at NASA, simulating what it would be like in space. Now here he was, 212,000 miles up, and his ship felt like a tomb. Without heat from the instruments, the temperature had dropped into the 50s. There were no lights and no machinery humming. He was a pilot without a ship, and he felt useless. He floated through the tunnel into the LEM, looked at Lovell and Haise, and said, "It's up to you now."

———◆———

Barbara Lovell had no idea what was happening in Apollo 13 when her mother appeared in her bedroom late Monday night. She had shut out the commotion downstairs—all the talking and the dreaded "Breaking News" on TV. But this time she didn't pretend to be asleep.

Her mother sounded calm enough when she spoke. "There's been an accident," she said. "They're bringing them home, but your dad's not walking on the moon."

Not walking on the moon. Barbara knew what a blow that would be for her father. All the weeks of training in Florida, the weeks visiting the spacecraft plants, the weeks of her childhood missed—it was all going to come to nothing. But at least he was coming home; her mother sounded confident of that. And that was enough for Barbara. She drifted off to sleep, a closed door, a landing, and a stairwell between her and the mounting stress downstairs.

If she had ventured beyond the landing, sleep might not have come so easily. Neighbors from the NASA community had been pouring in the door. Ashtrays and half-drunk cups of coffee littered the living room. By 11 p.m., all the TV stations were reporting the crisis.

"The Apollo 13 spacecraft has suffered a major electrical failure," announced ABC's Jules Bergman.

The astronaut families knew they could trust Bergman to get all the technical details right. But there was something harsh and gloomy about the way he delivered the news.

"Apollo 13 is apparently also losing breathing oxygen and the astronauts may have to use the LEM's oxygen supply," he continued. "The emergency has ruled out any chance of a lunar landing and could endanger the lives of the astronauts themselves."

Walter Cronkite, on CBS, was usually calm and comforting, but even he sounded grim. Around midnight, he declared, "This is indeed the gravest emergency probably yet in the American space program."

On her visit upstairs, Barbara's mother had done what parents do—what she'd been doing for eight years as a navy pilot's spouse and eight more as an astronaut's spouse. She tried to make her kids feel like their world was safe, like it was just another day at the office, and Dad would be home soon.

Walter Cronkite reports on an earlier Apollo mission on CBS.

Her job done, Marilyn Lovell went back downstairs, stared at the TV, and occasionally tried to talk to friends. When she couldn't stand it anymore she went into the bathroom and closed the door behind her. Then she kneeled on the floor and prayed.

CHAPTER 8

FREE RETURN

At Mission Control, Glynn Lunney had no time for prayer. But as he watched the systems go down in the command module, he had a moment of darkness deeper than any he'd felt before. He'd been watching over space flights for ten years, as a controller and a flight director. Never had he felt like this—the solid ground yanked from under his feet and his stomach dropping into the dark hole below. *Holy s___*, he thought to himself, *this is really happening.* He had three astronauts drifting in space, and the one vehicle that could get them back into Earth's atmosphere was as dead as a toy with no batteries.

The stress had been leaking into his voice since he took over from Kranz; if his controllers wavered for a second on the loop, he snapped at them. But stress was one thing, and despair was another. To work a problem, you had to believe there was a solution.

Fall back on your training and work the problem.

He could feel himself climbing out of that hole and back to his work. In the Trench below, the controllers were glued to their screens or deep in conversation on their headsets. No one seemed to have noticed his moment in hell.

Lunney pulled himself together and turned to the next task: getting the spacecraft on a course for home.

———————

How exactly were they going to get a crippled spacecraft back to Earth from 215,000 miles away? In the early hours of Tuesday morning, that decision rested in Gene Kranz's lap. Since Kranz handed over the headset to Lunney, he'd been consulting with the controllers and the other flight directors. In between discussions, he paced the floor with sweaty palms. That's how he knew the stress was building. Mentally, he stayed calm and direct and focused, but his body betrayed him. His controllers all joked about it: You knew things were getting tense when Kranz leaned on a desk full of papers and left a handprint behind.

Sweaty palms or no, with the astronauts settled in the

LEM, it was time to make a final call on the path home. There were two options, and neither was good. Kranz could call for a direct abort, in which they would use the giant engine in the service module to turn on a dime and rocket the spacecraft back to Earth. That had the advantage of getting the astronauts back fast—in about 34 hours. The other choice was to follow a "free return" course, in which the crew would fly around the moon and use its gravity to slingshot them back to Earth. On their current schedule, that would take nearly 100 hours.

Before the White Team went off duty, Kranz had some of his controllers begging him to turn the spacecraft around immediately. At current usage levels, it looked like the LEM would run out of power in less than 70 hours. More critically, water would be gone in about a day and a half. And without water, they had no way to cool the instruments. The guidance system would overheat like a stalled car in the desert.

It was hard to resist turning the crew around and getting them home as fast as possible. But the risks were huge. The moon's gravity was growing stronger by the minute. It would take a massive engine burn to bring a 100,000-pound spacecraft from 2,000 miles an hour to a dead stop, and then send it in the opposite direction. The only engine powerful enough to do it was located in the service module, not far from the oxygen tanks. One of those tanks may well have exploded into tiny bits of metal three hours ago. There was no way to tell if that engine was still intact. If they tried the direct abort and the engine quit early, they could slow Apollo 13 just enough for the moon's gravity to suck it in and send it plummeting to the lunar surface.

Before he had even left the console, Kranz had made up his mind. He turned to Lunney and said, "Our only real option is to go around the moon."

Now he gave the final okay for free return. They would just have to stretch two days' worth of power, oxygen, and water into four. Kranz headed downstairs where he had sent his White Team to work the problem. Each of his controllers would be asking for power—power to keep the guidance system running, power to get the command module back up, power to keep the crew alive. They were like castaways on a desert island clamoring for shares of a dwindling food supply. He needed someone to listen to them all and ration power. Someone to decide what was essential and what was not. Someone who knew the spacecraft inside and out. Someone who could make the impossible possible.

TO THE MOON—AND BACK?

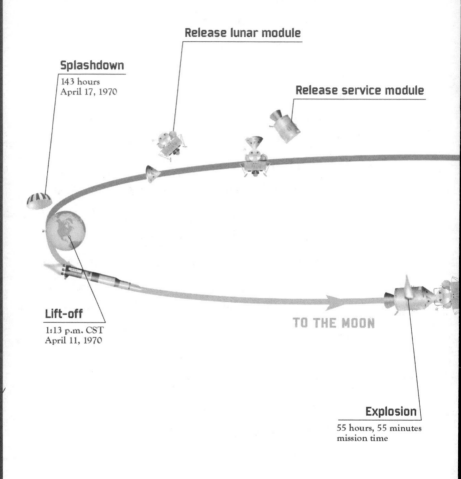

Release lunar module

Splashdown
143 hours
April 17, 1970

Release service module

Lift-off
1:13 p.m. CST
April 11, 1970

TO THE MOON

Explosion
55 hours, 55 minutes
mission time

Kranz and his team decided that a direct abort was too risky. They chose the longer option—a free-return course around the moon and back to Earth. With a blast from the engine to speed up the spacecraft as it leaves lunar orbit, they hoped they could get Apollo 13 back in 143 hours.

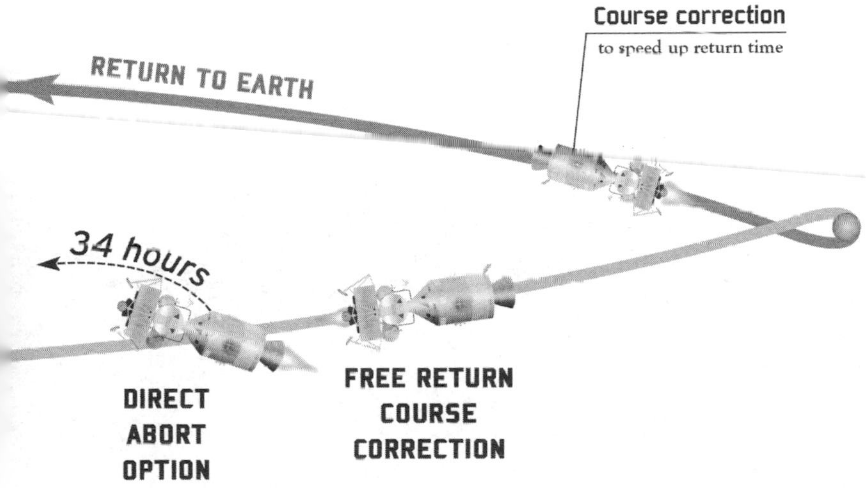

Course correction
to speed up return time

RETURN TO EARTH

34 hours

DIRECT
ABORT
OPTION

FREE RETURN
COURSE
CORRECTION

John Aaron was in Room 210 with the White Team controllers when Kranz walked in. Aaron was a twenty-seven-year-old EECOM with a well-earned reputation as an engineering genius. Where other people saw a jumble of unrelated numbers, he saw patterns. And where there were patterns, there were answers—clues that helped him diagnose problems long before anyone else knew what was happening.

A little after 9 p.m. that night, Aaron had been home getting ready to go in to NASA for his shift. He was

John Aaron (standing, in dark suit) started working at Mission Control during the Gemini missions, when he was just twenty-one years old.

shaving when his boss called and told him they thought they were having an instrumentation problem on the spacecraft. Aaron had asked him to go around to the consoles and read him numbers from all the systems. He knew before he got off the phone—there was no way it was just the gauges.

"I'll be right in," he said, "but in the meantime, you tell the guys that that's not an instrumentation failure. There's something really going on there."

Aaron got dressed, jumped in the car, and rushed to NASA. He was the extra "brain power" Kranz had been hoping for to back up Liebergot in the first hour of the crisis.

Now he had joined the White Team in 210, a big, ugly cavern of a room with no windows and a few gray tables scattered around. The smell of stale coffee and tobacco smoke clouded the air. Men sat on the floor and on tables, staring at orange printouts full of numbers. Some were trying to figure out what had gone wrong with the mission; others were deep into the task of saving it.

When Kranz walked in, he got everyone's attention.

"Okay, team, we have a hell of a problem," he said. "We are on the long return around the moon and it is our job to figure out how to get them home. From now on, the White Team is off-line."

They were the behind-the-scenes brain trust—the people who would figure out the procedures and feed them to the controllers on duty in the mission room. They had three problems to solve: 1) how to get the astronauts home as quickly as possible with only the LEM to navigate and propel the ship; 2) how to stretch the LEM's resources twice as far as they were meant to go; 3) how to start up the command module cold and use it for the final leg back to Earth.

Aaron knew the resources in the spacecraft as well as anyone, and he had one thought as he listened to Kranz speak: It just wasn't possible. Right about then, he heard Kranz call his name.

"John Aaron will be in charge of the spacecraft resources," Kranz announced. "Whatever he says goes. He has absolute veto authority over any use of our consumables."

And just like that, Aaron was thrown into the most important work he'd ever done. He was the power broker—the guy who would decide what could be used on the spacecraft and what couldn't, what they would shut down and what they would keep running. It wasn't that long since Aaron had been a teenager, fixing tractors on his parents' farm in Oklahoma. Now it was his job to keep a crippled spacecraft running so that three men didn't die in outer space.

Aaron decided he would have to think differently. If it looked impossible from where he sat, he would just have to enter the problem from the other end. He would assume it was possible and ask, what do you have to do to make it so?

"Okay, listen up." Kranz was finishing his pep talk. "When you leave this room, you must leave believing that this crew is coming home. I don't give a damn about the odds and I don't give a damn that we've never done anything like this before. Flight control will never lose an American in space."

———◆———

Jim Lovell had no intention of being lost in outer space. But right now, that's the way his spacecraft was headed, 30,000 miles from the moon and closing in fast. He stood in the LEM, pistol-grip controllers in hand, trying to convince himself he could pilot his way onto a new path—one that pointed in the opposite direction.

The problem was this: On previous Apollo flights, the astronauts started on a free-return trajectory. "Free" and "return"; those were comforting words. If anything went wrong, all the crew had to do was stay on course. The moon's gravity would do the work for them. It would bend their course in a broad arc, a hundred-some-odd miles from the lunar surface, whip them around the moon, and send them straight back to Earth.

As luck would have it, Apollo 13 had a different landing site than the two previous moon shots. To bring the spacecraft in close to the site, Mission Control had plotted a different course. If the astronauts did nothing to redirect themselves, they would miss the Earth by thousands of miles on the way back. Lovell, Haise, and Swigert would end up in permanent orbit with the Earth on one end and the moon on the other.

Anything but that.

When Lovell first trained as an astronaut, he had spent hours gazing at the moon. Just getting there, he thought, would be so overwhelming that you wouldn't worry about coming back. Now all he wanted to do was get the spacecraft pointed toward Earth, even if they never made it back to the surface. Burning up in the atmosphere would be better than getting stuck in space forever.

Plotting courses in space was a job for math geniuses. They balanced the speed of the spacecraft against the force of gravity. Approach the moon too slow and gravity fights your forward motion and pulls you in. Approach too fast and you soar around the moon until gravity loses its grasp and sends you hurtling off into space. Get it exactly right and you nestle into a perfect orbit or settle onto a course headed straight for home.

The calculations were so complex they were impossible for the average person to imagine. But the geniuses had it worked out. Under normal circumstances, Lovell wouldn't have to work that hard to get Apollo 13 back on a free-return course. He and Haise and Swigert would listen to the engineers in Houston and punch a set of coordinates into the computer. The thrusters would automatically position the spacecraft in the right orientation, or "attitude," in space. Once the ship was aligned the right way, they would punch another set of numbers into the computer and push a button. The engine would fire for exactly the right amount of time, and just like that, they'd be on a course for home.

But Lovell had given up on "normal" three hours ago. Nothing from here on in was going to be easy. For one thing, they weren't entirely sure where they were in space. The CSM had a guidance platform programmed into its computer—a kind of GPS that pinpointed where the spacecraft was in the sky relative to the stars. Just before they powered down, they had transferred the platform to the LEM. But they couldn't be sure it was exact enough to pull off a free-return burn. Houston wanted them to locate a couple of stars to fine-tune their platform.

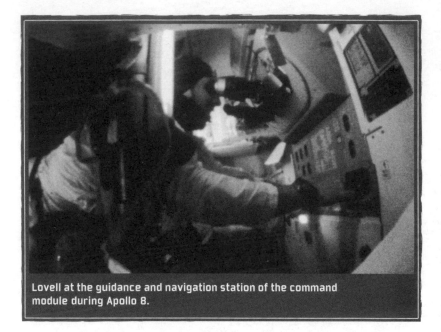
Lovell at the guidance and navigation station of the command module during Apollo 8.

So much for the most advanced technology known to humankind. Navigating by the stars was an ancient process that hadn't changed much since 19th-century mariners made their way across the ocean in sailing ships. And anyway, it didn't look to Lovell like it was going to work.

"Aquarius, Houston." It was Lousma on the air-ground loop. "Can you see any stars out the LEM window?"

Right now, it was so cold in the LEM that their breath had condensed into beads of water everywhere. They couldn't see a thing.

"We'll have to wipe them off, Jack," said Haise. "They're coated with water."

"Can I get a towel?" Lovell asked Haise.

He wiped off his window and peered out the left side of the LEM, but the sun was too bright. Not a single star was visible.

He switched places with Haise and cleared the right-side window. Tiny shards of light glimmered at him by the thousands. Most of them were recognizable—as pieces of his own spacecraft. Somewhere out there were constellations he would know from hours of study. But countless pieces of metal from the explosion blocked his view. Not only had the blast crippled the command module, it had stolen their oldest and most effective way of navigating in space.

"Okay," Lovell said. "I'm looking out of Fred's window. I see a lot of particles out there . . . so a lot of it is flashing in the local vicinity, and I don't recognize any constellations right now."

"Okay, Jim," Lousma said. "If that status changes, please let us know."

Lovell turned back to the more immediate task: learning how to pilot his ship from the LEM. Technically, Haise was the LEM pilot, and he knew more about the ship than anyone. But when it came time to fly, the mission commander took the controls, and the LEM pilot served as copilot. That time had arrived. Lovell returned to the left side of the cockpit and grabbed the two pistol-grip controllers—known in NASA-speak as the TTCA, or Thrust/ Translation Controller Assembly. The LEM had thrusters on the outside, pointing in all directions just like the CSM. But they were only meant to maneuver the LEM by itself, from lunar orbit to the moon's surface and back. Lovell had practiced it that way for hours in the simulator. Now he was dragging the entire CSM along with them—63,400 pounds of metal and fuel. It was as though he were trained to drive a pickup truck and someone had suddenly attached a 36-foot-long trailer to it.

———◆———

Glynn Lunney and everyone else on the air-ground loop got an earful as Lovell struggled to get control of the spacecraft. Normally, the astronauts switched off their connection to the ground when they talked among themselves. But in the heat of the moment they'd left their headsets on the "vox" setting that transmitted everything to Houston. And since NASA shared all communications with the public, every word went out, not just to the controllers but to reporters as well.

"I can't take that doggone roll out," Lovell said.

"Wait a minute," Haise said. "Do you fight roll by using the TTCA left right? That's what you need to play with."

"Okay, we'll try that. Let me get around, though—let it roll all the way."

"You can't let it roll all the way."

"I know, I know."

Lunney was only half-listening, but he didn't love what he heard. If he could help it, he didn't want the entire world to hear NASA's astronauts fumbling in the dark.

"You might let them know we're copying the vox, Jack," he said into the flight director's loop.

"Watch the crapping attitude," they heard Haise bark.

"We're okay," Lovell said.

"And Aquarius, Houston," Lousma cut in. "We've got you both on vox."

"You want us on vox, Jack?" Lovell asked, missing the point entirely.

"We have you on vox," Lousma said. "We're reading you loud and clear."

Lunney didn't give it another thought. He had come back from the dark hole of fear that nearly consumed him earlier. Now he was all business. At the rate they were going, the spacecraft would run out of water 40 hours before their earliest possible landing time. Lunney needed to get the crew on a free-return path as quickly as possible so he could start shutting down systems in the LEM.

At 1:35 a.m., four-and-a-half hours after the accident, Lousma got on the line. "Okay," he said to the crew. "We'd like to brief you on what our plan is. We're at this time water critical in the LEM. So we'd like to use as little as possible . . . So how do you feel about making a 16-foot-per-second burn in 37 minutes?"

Burn the LEM's engines for 16 seconds. That's all it would take to get them on a free-return course. But Lovell still hadn't been able to identify a single star to check his alignment. And he wasn't at all confident that the LEM's thrusters could maneuver the entire spacecraft as precisely as they needed to. "Well, we'll give it a try, Jack, if that's all we've got . . . Could you give us a little more time?"

In the spacecraft, they needed every second they could get. Readying the LEM normally took two hours. Haise did it in one, racing through his checklist, taking orders from the ground, flipping circuit breakers and punching numbers into the computer.

When he wasn't needed for the checklist, Lovell worked his controllers. Little by little, he started to get a feel for the unwieldy hulk of a spaceship. But no matter where he maneuvered, his flock of glimmering debris followed.

Haise peered out his window and reported to Lousma, "There are about a thousand false stars out here left over from some of the debris. It's hard to discern what's real and not real."

They would just have to take their chances that the guidance platform was good. The burn was supposed to put them 130 miles from the moon at their closest approach. That didn't leave much room for error.

With 10 minutes to go, Lovell maneuvered the ship into the precise position. Then he pressed a button, and the computer took over, holding the ship in place.

Lovell couldn't hear him, but on the ground in Houston, Lunney was still looking for assurance that the spacecraft was pointed in the right direction.

"Guidance, Flight," he said. "You got anything on confirming the attitude?"

"Negative, Flight."

"Is the judgment that it's okay to use?" Lunney asked.

"Roger."

With just over a minute to go, Lunney did his final checks.

"Guidance, okay?" he asked.

"We're good, Flight."

"CONTROL?"

"We're okay, Flight."

"TELMU?"

"We're Go, Flight."

"INCO, okay?"

"We're good, Flight."

"We're good here at one minute," Lunney announced.

"Roger, Aquarius, you're Go for the burn," Lousma reported to the crew.

Lovell gripped his throttle. On the console in front of him, a display flashed the numbers 99:40, code for "Do you really want to do this?" Lovell put his finger on the button and pushed.

"We have ignition, low throttle point," announced Hal Loden, the controller in charge of the LEM engines.

Lovell pushed his throttle forward, and the computer brought the engine to 40 percent.

"Rates look good," said Loden.

"Okay, Aquarius, you're looking good," Lousma announced.

Lovell waited. Thirty seconds ticked past, and the computer shut down the engine right on target.

"Auto shutdown," he announced.

For 20 seconds, he waited for word from the ground. At the very least they would have to "trim" their course—fire the thrusters to make a small correction in their path. But Lousma's voice came through loud and clear.

"Okay," he said, "you're Go in the residuals, proceed."

Haise could barely believe it. "When you say Go on the residuals, you mean don't trim them. Is that right?"

"That's affirmative," replied Lousma. "No trim required."

For the first time in five and half hours, Lovell felt himself relax. They had used the LEM's engine to guide the entire spacecraft—and it worked. If they did nothing else the rest of the trip, chances were good they would still end up in Earth orbit.

Haise worked for a while, powering down whatever he could in the LEM. Then he looked at his watch. It was after 3 a.m. Tuesday morning. The last six hours had passed in a dream. On the one hand, he couldn't believe it had been that long. And yet the smooth, easy hours of his first two days in space seemed like another era entirely. All of a sudden he felt exhausted, drained from the urgency of the last few hours. He was happy when Houston radioed up with a plan for the lunar module pilot to get some sleep. Haise drifted into the cold command module, climbed into a thin sleeping sack, and closed his eyes.

Swigert, meanwhile, stayed in the lunar module with Lovell. Since the command module went dark, his two crewmates had done most of the technical tasks. But Swigert had found plenty of grunt work to do. He had brought water in from the command module in plastic bags and moved things around to make more room. Now time began to slow, and his mind wandered. A free-return course sounded great, but they were still headed away from Earth in a ship that might or might not have enough power to get them all the way home. It was a very real possibility that they would never set foot on their planet again. He couldn't help thinking how your life can hinge on the littlest things—things you have no control over. Charlie Duke, the astronaut who exposed them all to the measles, just happened to go to a picnic with a sick kid. If he'd gone out for a burger instead, Ken Mattingly would be up here right now, and Swigert would be watching from the ground.

As the morning wore on, Swigert kept watch out the window. Every now and then he caught sight of the Earth. The planet was beautiful, gleaming blue and white against the blackened sky. But it also looked about the size of a quarter. And for now, it was getting smaller by the minute.

CHAPTER 9

TRAPPED

When Barbara Lovell woke up on Tuesday morning, her father was 15,000 miles from the moon and still pointed away from Earth. One look out the window and she knew that whatever had happened up there, it was big news. Reporters swarmed like bees outside the house. Broadcast trucks lined the circle at the end of the driveway. Men and women crowded their lawn, notebooks and pens in hand. Cameras and microphones were everywhere, ready to be shoved in someone's face.

The mob actually hadn't been around much since the launch on Saturday. Apollo 13 was the *third* moon mission, after all, and the newspapers figured no one cared anymore. But now that her father was in trouble, everyone wanted a glimpse of the anxious family. Barbara's mother was disgusted. *Where were the reporters yesterday when things were going fine?* she wanted to know. When NASA asked if the news stations could build a broadcast tower on the lawn, Marilyn Lovell said absolutely not.

She also decided that Barbara wasn't going to school. That was fine with Barbara; at least she wouldn't have to face the microphones. But as the day wore on, the house started to feel like a prison. She wanted to talk to her friends, especially Connie. But the protocol officers with their NASA pins and their Secret-Service stone faces were screening her calls. She knew Connie was trying to get through, and they kept saying Barbara wasn't available. Protecting her from the reporters was one thing, but what right did they have to keep her from her own friends?

Barbara felt trapped and alone. She still didn't know how worried she should be, but she'd been picking up bits of information from the TV: *an accident . . . using the lunar module . . . running low on power.* The announcers held up little models of the spaceship while they explained how her father was going to make it home.

The mood around the house told her more than anything else. People came and went, mostly her mother's friends. In the morning there were a dozen people in the family room, and judging from the mess, it looked like there had been a lot more the night before. During the day they paced around like zombies, talking in low voices. Generally, they left her mother alone.

Marilyn Lovell had barely slept the night before, and she looked exhausted. From time to time she would huddle over the "squawk box"—a little speaker the size of an electric pencil sharpener that broadcast Barbara's dad's voice live from space. It was against NASA rules for family members to speak directly to the spacecraft, so this was all they had. Mostly it sounded like static, and the language the crew spoke was so full of technical gibberish that Barbara rarely bothered to listen. But to her mom, it was

The Squawk Box: Barbara's mother listens for word from Apollo 13 while Jeffrey vies for her attention.

a lifeline. When Marilyn Lovell wasn't watching TV or listening to the astronauts, she walked around in a daze, looking like her mind was 200,000 miles away.

———◆———

At 7 a.m. Houston time, Jim Lovell had gotten even less sleep than his wife. For ten hours now, he'd been managing one crisis after another. Some of the pressure had lifted after the free-return burn. But since then he'd been working to power down the LEM. He'd also been wrestling with the thrusters to get the ship rotating so the sun didn't overheat one side and freeze the other. And all the while, Houston couldn't seem to get the doggone communications working right.

Joe Kerwin had taken over the CAPCOM seat from Jack Lousma, and half the time Lovell couldn't hear a word he was saying.

"Houston, Aquarius," Lovell said. "How do you read me?"

"Aquarius, this is Houston." Kerwin said. "We read you with a lot of static—"

"We read you with a lot of noise," Lovell said. "It seems better now, do you read us better?"

"Uh, I didn't copy your last remark, Jim. I heard that you had a lot of noise in the background also."

That was a typical conversation, and each one seemed to end with Kerwin saying, "Hold on while we evaluate it," or "Stand by while we think about it."

Finally, at around 8:30 a.m., Lovell got a break from the static and the fruitless back and forth. Houston had no instructions for the next hour. With no one ordering him to throw circuit breakers or fire thrusters, Lovell let his tired mind wander. If nothing had gone wrong, he and Fred Haise would be landing on the moon tomorrow. But everything had gone wrong, and now it wasn't just their mission at stake. It had taken the space program a year and a half to recover from the fire on Apollo 1. Who knew how long it would take them to recover from this disaster.

"Well," he said to Swigert, "I'm afraid it's going to be the last lunar mission for a long time."

It didn't take long for Lovell to stop speculating and get back to work. At the rate they were traveling, the LEM was going to run out of power no matter how many systems they shut down. To get them back to Earth faster, Houston was planning another burn just after they rounded the moon, at 79 hours mission time. That was 10 hours from now. The idea was to fire the LEM engine again, this time long enough to give the spacecraft a powerful boost. But they'd be nearing the moon in just a few hours, and he still had no details.

How big a burn did they have in mind? How was he going to make sure they were aligned properly? And how severely would they have to power down the LEM after the burn was over?

Before he went to sleep, Haise had done some quick calculations of his own about the LEM's power supply. The guidance system had been burning through cooling water for 11 hours now—and they still had 10 to go before they could power down. Haise had originally thought they would run out of water five hours before splashdown.

Lovell and Swigert were trying to remember Haise's numbers when the lunar module pilot himself poked his head through the tunnel and into the LEM.

"Come on in, Freddo," Swigert said. "Did you sleep good?"

Haise answered by asking for some aspirin. Normally, he could sleep through anything, but it had been a fitful five hours. The command module was cold, and with the tunnel open, you could hear everything that happened in the LEM. All he had to show for his rest time was a splitting headache.

At 11 a.m. Houston time, Lovell and Swigert tried to put all the questions behind them. The burn was nine hours away; Houston would figure it out. They left the

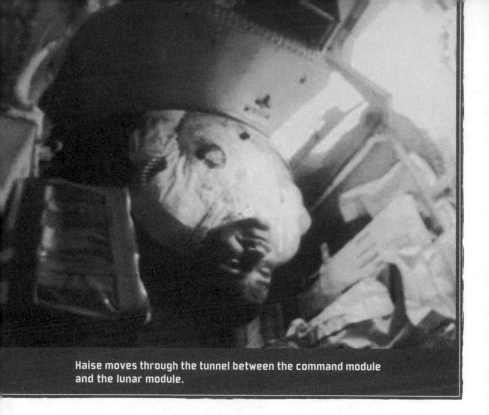

Haise moves through the tunnel between the command module and the lunar module.

lunar module to Haise and drifted through the tunnel to the darkened command module, hoping to get some sleep.

———◆———

At Mission Control, the night had passed with no sleep for anyone. Ashtrays served as paperweights for printouts full of numbers. Coffeepots were drained and put back on their burners, filling the air with the smell of something scorched. When the sun came up, Gene Kranz was prowling the halls of the second floor, directing traffic, while John Aaron and the rest of the White Team figured out how to run the ship on a starvation diet. Glynn Lunney, still on duty as flight director, shepherded the spacecraft through the hours after the free-return burn. By the early hours of the morning, the other two flight directors and their teams had all arrived at work. They gathered in knots behind the consoles, checking numbers from the back rooms, scribbling notes on worn-out pads of paper, and debating the next big decision: how to get the ship home as quickly and safely as possible.

By 10:30 a.m., the flight directors had all agreed on the best option. During any other mission that would be

On Duty: Controllers gather around the flight director's console, debating how to get the ship back to Earth.

enough: debate ended, decision made, no one else to answer to. On this mission, there was too much at stake for it to be that easy. This time, they would have to answer to the highest levels of NASA leadership.

If Lovell, Haise, and Swigert didn't come home, they would become the first human beings ever to die in space. And the entire world would be watching. Newspapers around the globe were already filling their front pages with news of the crisis. People in New York City had woken that morning to a giant headline in the *New York Times*: "POWER FAILURE IMPERILS ASTRONAUTS; APOLLO WILL HEAD BACK TO EARTH." Anyone with a TV got to follow the drama *live*. They had no video from the spacecraft; the crew couldn't afford to waste precious power or time sending broadcasts back to Earth. But everything the astronauts said on the voice loop went out to the world. That included Lovell's off-hand prediction that NASA would not be launching moon missions for a long time to come.

At 10:30 a.m. on Tuesday, April 14, the flight directors climbed up to the VIP room overlooking Mission Control. Two dozen NASA executives were gathered exactly where Barbara Lovell and her family had sat for the TV broadcast just 14 hours ago.

Gerald Griffin, the Gold Team flight director, presented

the options to the bosses. Obviously, he said, they wanted to get the crew home as quickly as possible. To do it, they could fire up the LEM's engine as the spacecraft came around the back side of the moon and blast it at full throttle for several minutes. That would get them back Thursday morning, 118 hours into the mission. The controllers in charge of consumables on the LEM loved this option. The LEM would only have to support the astronauts for 37 hours after the burn—until they powered up the command module for reentry. The way they were figuring now, that would leave them with power, water, and oxygen to spare.

All that breathing room would feel like a big relief—but it would come at a cost. The massive burn would eat up nearly all the fuel available to the LEM's engine; the crew would have precious little to spare if they had to make course corrections later on. And that wasn't the only sacrifice required. To get the spacecraft up to speed, they would have to lighten their load by ditching the 50,000-pound service module.

At first glance, that didn't seem like much of a hardship. The service module had been nothing but dead weight since the accident. But it was protecting a critical piece of the command module—a piece that could either deliver the astronauts safely into the ocean or burn them alive

60 miles from home. Nestled under the service module, on the wide base of *Odyssey*'s cone, was the 3-inch-thick heat shield. The heat shield was built to resist 5,000 degrees' worth of friction as the command module burrowed through Earth's atmosphere. But no one knew whether it could survive a day and a half exposed to the freezing-cold temperatures of space. Did anyone really want to find out now?

The alternative to the super-fast burn, Griffin explained to his audience, was a gentle nudge. The controllers had worked out a burn that would speed up the ship a mere 600 miles per hour. The crew could keep their service module and plenty of fuel to nurse them back on course as they neared the Earth. The trade-off was that they wouldn't make it home until Friday noon, at 142 hours mission time.

When Griffin finished, the flight directors left the bosses to talk it over. The NASA bigwigs debated for an hour, weighing the unknown dangers of the fast return with the known dangers of the slower option. It didn't take long for them to agree on the slow route home.

The flight directors breathed a sigh of relief. Griffin turned to Lunney and said, "What do you say we quit talking about this thing and see if we can go do it."

After the burn, the rest would be up to John Aaron and his engineers. Somehow, they would have to make the limited resources of the LEM last another 61 hours. For the crew that meant 61 hours in a ship without a guidance platform, 61 hours in cramped quarters without heat, and 61 hours in which the command module could freeze beyond their ability to bring it back to life.

CHAPTER 10

AROUND THE MOON

On Tuesday afternoon, Barbara Lovell might as well have been trapped in a spaceship. Jeffrey had gone to preschool, so she didn't have to watch him. Her friends hadn't been able to get through the wall of secrecy put up by the NASA gatekeepers downstairs. And the mob of reporters still stood guard outside.

In the past, Barbara had hatched escape plans worthy of a spy. On the Gemini flights, when she was still growing quickly, the reporters didn't recognize her from mission to mission. She'd walk out the door and tell them she was Barbara Lovell's friend. After they figured it out, they would meet her at the school bus stop in the afternoon. *Hey, stop the presses, Barbara Lovell's coming home from school!* To give them the slip, Barbara started getting off the bus early, at the circle where the Glenns and the Carpenters lived. Then she'd walk home the back way,

Trapped: Barbara didn't leave the house during the first day of the crisis.

along the canal that ran behind the houses on Lazywood Lane. Sometimes, when people came to pick her up, she'd sneak out the side of the house to the driveway and hide on the floor in the back of the car.

When she escaped, her favorite place to go was Connie's house. It was a delicious refuge from the reporters and the Secret Service guys and the people coming and going. She'd slip out the back door and walk along the canal through the Benwares' yard next door. Once she was out of range of the cameras, she'd make her way to the road and walk to Connie's—free from it all. It was so calm and peaceful there. They'd go to the grocery store or the pool. If Connie's dad was around he might take them waterskiing.

Connie, on the other hand, couldn't get enough of Barbara's house during the missions. The people and the noise and the TV and the squawk box; all of it was exciting to her. Of course, she didn't have to worry about the reporters, but she probably wouldn't have minded the attention. The best part for Connie were the days before the flights, when the gifts arrived. An endless stream of stuff just appeared at the door. For free! When the doorbell rang, she and Barbara could go see what they'd gotten: stockings and dresses and specialty foods. Once they got a case of seasoned salt—with the Lovell name on the labels.

Barbara needed Connie now, and she had asked her mother to call off the Secret Service guys. Her mom was surrounded by friends; why shouldn't she have her friends too?

The message must have gotten through because at some point, she heard footsteps on the stairs. Connie appeared in her doorway. She had taken the escape route in reverse—back by the canal and in the back door. It was great to have her there. She didn't seem worried about Barbara's dad, but she had definitely noticed a change in the mood downstairs. It wasn't like the other missions where people laughed and mixed drinks at the bar between the kitchen and the family room. This time, it just felt dark and somber down there.

———◆———

With the TV on downstairs, Barbara's mother and the neighbors who packed themselves into the family room got more news than they needed. From time to time, they sat through special reports from Lazywood Lane—*Live, from the Lovells' front yard!* It was a strange, out-of-body experience, like watching yourself on a surveillance camera in a store.

Look, there's Jeffrey and a friend going off to preschool with their NASA caps on their heads.

Look, there are the neighbors arriving with a casserole.

"Here in the astronaut compound," declared the CBS reporter, "a spirit of togetherness prevails."

That may have been true, but he didn't figure it out from speaking to Marilyn Lovell. Barbara's mom refused to talk to the reporters. A friend had shepherded Jeffrey out the door to the car in the morning while she stayed inside with the TV and the squawk box.

Most of the news announcers were optimistic. NASA reported that the water, power, and oxygen supply looked good. They were confident that the burn, scheduled for 8:40 p.m., would get the crew home with time to spare.

But when you listened closely, there were always *ifs*: *If* the LEM engine performed the way it was supposed to; *if* the alignment of the spacecraft was good; *if* the command module could be powered up effectively; *if* the heat shield wasn't damaged.

In the afternoon, Glynn Lunney sat at a news conference answering questions about his night's work at the flight director's console. Eventually they asked him point blank, "Are the astronauts safe?"

"Well, uh," he said. Then he hesitated and cleared his throat. "They're safe in the sense that, uh, we have the situation stabilized, uh, we think . . . We just have to continue to keep it that way."

You couldn't take much comfort in a response like that.

Before the burn, a priest arrived at the Lovells' house to lead everyone in a communion service. Not long after, they'd be joined by people praying all across the country. Congress had passed a resolution asking every American to pause at 8 p.m. Houston time and pray for the safe return of the astronauts.

———◦———

At 6 p.m. the sun hung low in the sky over the Lovell house. Two hundred and forty thousand miles away, Jim

Father Donald Raish leads Barbara's mother and friends in prayer on Tuesday afternoon.

Lovell gazed out the tiny window of his spacecraft at a sunset of his own. They were 1,000 miles from the moon and closing in at 4,000 miles per hour. The sun had slowly disappeared over the lunar horizon. It was nighttime on the moon, and the sky was breathtaking.

"Man, look at those stars," Lovell said into the voice loop. "We are in the shadow of the moon now. The sun is just about set as far as I can see and the stars are all coming out."

"Okay," said the CAPCOM from the dingy control room in Houston. "And if you are ready to copy, we have LOS/AOS times for you."

Vance Brand, the CAPCOM on duty, was not interested in the sublime beauty of space travel. In just 25 minutes, Apollo 13 would disappear around the back side of the moon. At that point they would lose all contact with Earth, a condition known in NASA-speak as LOS, or Loss of Signal. Twenty-five minutes after that, they would reappear on the other side of the moon, reaching AOS, or Acquisition of Signal. Then they would prepare for the burn.

At 77:08 mission time, the spacecraft drifted out of contact with Earth. The air-ground loop went dead. For eight minutes they floated in a cave. The moon's gravity held them in a tight loop, less than 150 miles away. And yet, the moon itself was nothing but a shadow, a looming blackness blotting out the stars.

Then, at 77:16, the sun appeared low on the lunar horizon. The gray, plastery, ancient surface of the moon suddenly burst into view. In the low-angled light, every crag cast a shadow. Every pockmark looked as though you could reach out and trace its contours with your finger.

Haise and Swigert were in awe. Yes, there was a burn to do in two hours. Yes, they still had to travel 240,000 miles in a crippled ship. Yes, there were several ways in which they could die in the next 65 hours. But who could

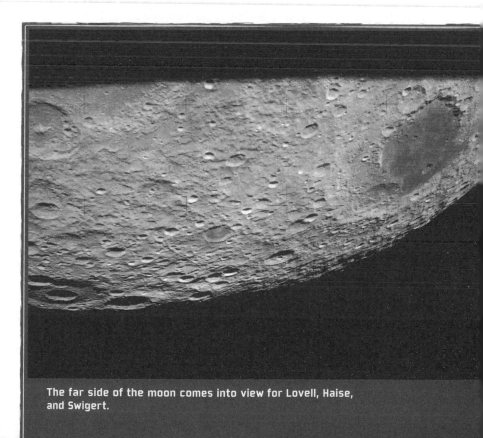

The far side of the moon comes into view for Lovell, Haise, and Swigert.

think about any of that right now? They pressed their faces to the windows and started taking pictures.

Only twelve human beings had experienced what they were seeing right now. The lunar surface filled their windows—no longer a ball hanging in space but a landscape below them. It was ancient terrain, scarred by craters millions, even billions, of years old. On Earth, weather and other forces renewed the surface constantly. Erosion wore down mountains while volcanic activity built them up again. The moon, on the other hand, had no atmosphere and therefore, no weather. Without wind and rain, its surface did not erode. Meteors had bombarded it for eons, and the scars never healed.

Lovell had moved aside so Haise and Swigert could get their fill at the windows. He had been here already, less than a year and a half ago on Apollo 8. He remembered the feeling. The view had transformed the crew—Borman, Anders, and Lovell—from grizzled test pilots to gaping tourists. The landscape looked like nothing he had seen before—bleak and colorless, like a vast abandoned battlefield.

"It certainly would not appear to be a very inviting place to live or work," Borman had said.

And yet, Lovell would have given anything to work there for a day. "If we could only get that scant 60 miles closer—really down there—" he told *Life* magazine after Apollo 8 returned, "then we'd have a chance to pry open some of the secrets of creation. The lunar surface was so close. It beckoned."

But for all the strange allure of the moon, it didn't compare to the sight that greeted Apollo 8 as it returned to the front side of the moon: the Earth rising over the lunar horizon. It looked as beautiful as anything Lovell had seen—the blue of the oceans, the browns of the land, the gleaming white of the clouds. It was the only spot of color in all the universe.

"There's a beautiful moon out there tonight," Houston had radioed up.

"There's a beautiful Earth out there," Frank Borman had replied, with awe in his voice.

People who walk Earth day in and day out don't appreciate what they have, Lovell had thought. From this far away you could see the planet for what it was—an oasis of life in a vast, empty sky. It looked so fragile; small enough to fit behind his thumb if he held out his arm. And yet it held the hopes and dreams and loves of more than three billion people. It held everything he had ever cared about.

Now, a year and a half later, he was back. At 77:34 mission time, 6:47 p.m. back in the Lovell living room,

Earthrise: Home as Lovell saw it from 240,000 miles away during Apollo 8.

the Earth rose for Apollo 13, and Lovell made contact with his home planet again.

"Aquarius, Houston," came the CAPCOM's voice. "How do you read?"

"Stand by for AOS," Lovell said. "Houston, Aquarius."

For a few minutes, Lovell played tour guide for Haise

and Swigert. He pointed out Smythii and Crisium, two broad lunar lowlands that were mislabeled "seas" by early astronomers. He told Haise to take a picture of the giant crater Tsiolkovsky.

Ten minutes later, Haise and Swigert were still glued to their windows, and Lovell had had enough. His crewmates were rookie astronauts; they might make it back here someday. Lovell, who had spent more time in space than anyone else, probably wouldn't be assigned another mission. The moon was out of reach for him, and it always would be. Out the window, that other globe—the beautiful blue one—was slowly getting bigger. They all needed to focus their attention in that direction, toward home.

"Okay, look," Lovell said, all trace of the friendly tour guide gone from his voice. "Let's get the cameras squared away; let's get all set to burn. We got one chance now."

"Okay," said Swigert.

"We're not going to hack it at 152 hours," Lovell added.

With no burn at all, that would be their total mission time. The burn would get them home 10 hours faster. It didn't sound like a lot, but every minute could turn out to be vital. Getting *almost* all the way back to Earth before they ran out of power wouldn't do anyone any good.

The ship passes over Tsiolkovsky Crater, named for the Russian scientist who first showed that space travel was possible.

They moved through the powerup checklist like experts this time. Haise punched the coordinates into the guidance computer. Once again, they were going without an exact alignment. Fifteen minutes before the burn, Brand told Lovell where the moon should line up outside his window. It was a crude but simple way to make sure they were pointed in the right direction. Lovell peered out and confirmed it was exactly where it should be. They were 6,000 miles away now, the moon back to a full circle in his window. But he could still make out the features. On the edge of the Sea of Tranquility, he saw a triangular peak he had identified and named during Apollo 8. He turned the air-ground loop on long enough to broadcast the news to Earth.

"I can even see Mount Marilyn," he said.

Who knows, maybe the TV reporters would pick up on the reference and decide it was worth a mention. If they did, it just might reach Marilyn Lovell, sitting in her family room hoping the burn would get her husband home.

Back in the control room, Gene Kranz and his White Team had taken over again. It would be their job to shepherd the crew through the burn. Dozens of people had wandered in for the event—controllers from the off-duty shifts, the head of NASA and the second-in-command, the crew that was scheduled for the next Apollo mission. About five minutes before the burn, Kranz went around the room and checked with each controller in turn. All systems looked good.

"Jim, you are GO for the burn," said Brand.

"Roger, I understand," said Lovell. "GO for the burn."

"One minute," Brand reported.

"Roger."

The astronauts felt the LEM's engines light behind them, and the ship edged forward. The acceleration pushed them toward the floor, and for the first time in three days of zero gravity, they felt like their bodies had weight.

"We're burning 40 percent," Lovell reported.

"Houston copies."

"One hundred percent," Lovell said.

The engine roared behind the ship.

"Aquarius, you were looking good at two minutes," said Brand. "Still looking good."

"Two minutes. Roger."

Three hundred miles an hour faster and still accelerating.

"Aquarius, you're GO at three minutes."

"Aquarius. Roger."

At exactly 4 minutes 15 seconds, the computer shut the engine down.

"Shutdown," Lovell announced.

"Roger, shutdown," said Brand.

Thirty seconds later, the verdict was in. They were on course and headed for a landing in the Pacific Ocean in 63 hours.

"Good burn, Aquarius," Brand said. Lovell couldn't hear or see the reaction in Houston, but all around Brand controllers were applauding and slapping one another on the back.

Lovell barely took a deep breath. He had slept only one hour in the last day and a half, but neither rest nor celebration were the first things on his mind.

"Roger," he said. "And now we want to power down as soon as possible."

CHAPTER 11

"MY DAD ISN'T COMING HOME"

By Wednesday morning, Apollo 13 was an oversized, flying refrigerator. The command module had been dead for 36 hours, warmed only by the heat that drifted in from the LEM. Now even the LEM had gone dark and frigid. After the burn, the crew had powered down to 12 amps, less than a quarter of the normal supply. The power in the LEM's system would barely keep three 100-watt lightbulbs lit.

The hardest part for Lovell had been to watch the guidance platform go down. Known as the PGNS, or "Pings" in NASA-speak, the Primary Guidance, Navigation and Control System was their GPS. It kept track of their position in space so they knew how to align themselves when they needed to change course. Lovell already knew they would have to make a midcourse correction before they made it home. When they did, they'd have to navigate completely by the stars—assuming they could see any.

"I sure hate to lose the PGNS," he had said to Houston, looking for reassurance. "I sure hope that procedure for the midcourse is a good one."

"It is," said the CAPCOM.

He failed to mention that Houston hadn't yet decided what the procedure would be.

At 1 a.m. Lovell decided he needed some sleep. He left the ship to Haise and Swigert and drifted into the command module—"the bedroom," they were calling it now. He zipped himself into his feather-light sleeping bag and curled into a ball. In zero gravity, air has no movement to it, so warm air doesn't rise. If you stay still enough, your own body heat wraps you in an insulating pocket that keeps the cold away.

At least that was the theory. But in a command module where the temperature had fallen well below 50 degrees, body heat wasn't enough. After an hour, Lovell was back in the LEM, where it was still a few degrees warmer.

Jack Lousma was back on as CAPCOM, 24 hours after he finished leading the crew through the early hours of the crisis. "Gee whiz," he said to Lovell. "You got up kind of early, didn't you?"

Lovell dozes in place in the lunar module after giving up on the frigid command module.

"It's cold back there in the command module," said Lovell.

The cold was only part of it, though. It was hard to sleep when so many issues remained unresolved. Houston still hadn't told Lovell how he was going to align the ship for course correction. And he couldn't be sure they were getting their thermal control right. The computer was rotating the ship to distribute the sun's heat evenly. But the way they were tumbling through space, it wasn't clear the procedure was working.

And the final thing keeping Lovell up? There was a chance that he and Swigert and Haise would suffocate on their own breath a few hours from now.

This was a problem Houston had been aware of for a while. With every breath the astronauts took, oxygen fed their cells to keep them alive. But just like on Earth, every time they breathed out, they filled the air with carbon dioxide, or CO_2. In a house or a building, the gas escapes without endangering anyone. But in a sealed spacecraft, it wouldn't take long for it to fill the air and poison everyone inside.

Both the LEM and the command module had special filters to trap the CO_2 and keep the air clean. But the LEM's filters, like everything else aboard the lunar lander, were only designed to support two men for two days.

Sometime in the late morning, those filters would fill with gas and lose their ability to soak up any more CO_2. Every breath would begin to poison the air. If they did nothing, the crew would start to feel light-headed. They'd get short of breath and their hearts would pound. Eventually, they would lose consciousness. The spacecraft would continue on, carrying their bodies toward home.

Everyone knew that the solution to the problem lay in the dead command module. *Odyssey* would be inactive for the better part of four days. It had plenty of extra CO_2 filters, known as lithium hydroxide canisters. But no one had ever thought they would be needed on the LEM. As a result, they'd been built in a completely different shape and size than the LEM's filters; they were square when they needed to be round. To keep the crew from suffocating, NASA had to figure out how to fit a square peg in a round hole.

Thankfully, that is exactly what they had done. A team of engineers gathered in Building 7 at NASA with all the materials the crew had available on the spacecraft. When they emerged, they had an odd-looking contraption pieced together with tape, cardboard, plastic bags, and an old sock—a makeshift machine designed to save the lives of three astronauts.

Deke Slayton, head of flight crew operations, explains the makeshift CO_2 filter in Mission Control.

By about 9:30 a.m. Houston time, Haise and Swigert had gotten a few hours' sleep. They gathered in the LEM with Lovell and got to work while Jack Lousma read up instructions from the ground. The men dug out a roll of duct tape and a towel. Lovell found some long underwear they were supposed to wear during the lunar landing. He unwrapped them and saved the plastic bags. Haise dug out a set of spiral-bound cards with instructions for lifting off from the lunar surface. He cut off one of the cards. If they couldn't use this stuff on the moon, it could at least help them get back to Earth.

For the next hour, they worked like preschool kids engrossed in a craft project. *Sticky side up or sticky side down? Which end is top and which is bottom? Don't cut the hole too big; we can always make it bigger.* Here they were, surrounded by the most advanced technology in the world—and they were making a filter out of an arm's-length of tape, some carved-up cardboard, and a piece of an old towel.

"Okay," said Swigert when their work was done. "Our do-it-yourself lithium-hydroxide canister change is complete."

Two hours later, Lovell had finally gone off to sleep. Haise hooked up the finished CO_2 filter and verified that it was doing its job. Then he thanked Lousma for all the work they were doing on the ground.

"We're just having a ball down here working on all kinds of new procedures, Fred," Lousma said. "We expect to have your entry procedures out here by Saturday or Sunday at the very latest."

"Saturday or Sunday?" said a groggy Haise, not entirely sure if Lousma was joking. They were supposed to land on Friday.

"At the very latest," replied Lousma in deadpan voice.

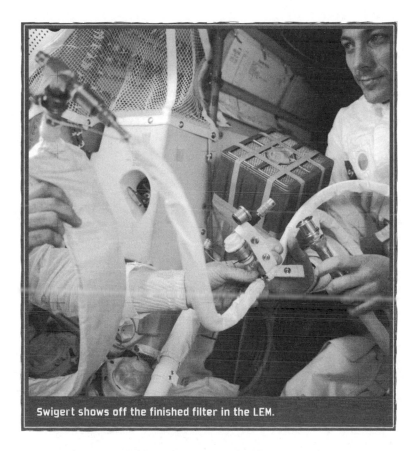
Swigert shows off the finished filter in the LEM.

"Take your time, Jack," said Haise.

It wasn't clear from the exchange just how much of a sense of humor Fred Haise had left.

———◆———

John Aaron, the "power broker" at Mission Control, knew time was in short supply. Huddled in Room 210 with his slide rule and his charts, he had to figure out how to start a freezing-cold command module in space with almost no power at all. No one had ever done it before. And the way NASA normally works, a procedure like this would take a month or two to develop, revise, and get approved. Aaron had 36 hours to get it done.

He figured that if he cut the systems on the command module down to their bare bones, the reentry batteries would provide him with two hours' worth of power. On the ground it took an entire day to start up the command module. Most of the controllers thought he was crazy to try it in two hours. Suppose the thrusters were frozen and wouldn't heat up in time? Suppose the wiring was wet from condensation and it shorted out an important circuit? If anything went wrong there would be no time to fix it.

But Aaron had no choice. He went from controller to controller, bargaining with each of them for power. The GNC in charge of the guidance systems wanted the cooling system up two and a half hours ahead of time. Aaron wanted to give it a half hour. They compromised at one and a half. The controller in charge of recovery operations in the ocean wanted a little locator beacon powered up so the ships could track the spacecraft if it landed off course. Aaron turned him down.

"Our biggest problem is getting them *to* an ocean," he said. "If we can get them there, surely you can find them."

Finally, on Wednesday night, Aaron stood in front of the controllers in Room 210 with a plan they weren't going to like. The only way they could get the command module powered up was to do it blind. The communications network that let Mission Control monitor the systems on the spacecraft took up too much power. They would have to leave it off until *Odyssey* was completely powered up.

"John, this is just asking for trouble," someone said.

"Doing it any other way is asking for more," he replied.

"But no one's ever tried this kind of thing before. No one's even *thought* of trying it."

"It won't be the first thing about this flight that's been irregular," Aaron said.

Someone else told him it was more than irregular; it was downright dangerous. "Suppose something starts to overheat or blow. We won't know until it's too late."

In John Aaron's view, that was a chance they would have to take.

———◆———

Barbara Lovell wasn't really sure *what* chances her father was taking. No one had sat her down and told her about frozen thrusters or damp wiring, and she hadn't asked. But she could feel the tension building in the house.

Her brother Jeffrey was too young to understand what was happening, and that was exactly how it should be. All he knew was that his dad wouldn't be bringing back the moon rock he'd promised him. He got over that disappointment soon enough.

For her younger sister, Susan, there was a lot more than moon rocks at stake. At school the day before, someone had come up to her and said, "I'm so sorry your dad isn't coming home." Then she came back to Lazywood Lane to find a priest in his black robes leading everyone in prayer. The scene looked way too much like a funeral service. That evening, their mother found Susan sobbing in her room. It took a lot of consoling to convince her that NASA knew exactly what they were doing. They would make sure she saw her dad again.

On Wednesday, Barbara finally got out of the house. The reporters caught up with her at the car before she could close the door. They fired questions at her while the cameras clicked. The pictures would make it into the newspapers the next morning: "Barbara Lovell, 16, daughter of Apollo 13 astronaut Jim Lovell, prepares to drive to school from family home."

Escape: Caught by reporters, Barbara tries to leave the house on Wednesday morning.

Later that day, she made her way to her sanctuary at Connie's house. The two friends made a run to the grocery store, but when they pulled into the parking lot, Barbara didn't get out. All the stress of the last two days churned inside her—the hushed conversations in the family room, the breaking news broadcasts, the rasp of the squawk box. Alone with Connie, she finally felt like she could let it all out. In the parking lot, surrounded by station wagons and abandoned shopping carts, she burst into tears.

"My dad isn't coming home," she sobbed. "I know I'm not going to see him again."

Connie, sitting three feet away, looked honestly shocked—like it was the first time she had considered that NASA, with its genius engineers, might fail to bring Barbara's dad home.

CHAPTER 12

DEEP FREEZE

If Barbara Lovell had been listening to the squawk box on Wednesday afternoon, she might have felt better. Fred Haise was alone in his lunar module while Swigert and Jim Lovell were getting some sleep. Haise was feeling good enough to turn to one of his favorite topics: food. He had barely eaten for a day after the accident. Now he was back on schedule, wrestling with a package of gingerbread cubes. To save water, the crew had stopped eating freeze-dried meals that needed to be mixed with liquid. That meant no more chicken and rice, or pork and scalloped potatoes. What they had left sounded like a set of flavored building blocks: coconut cubes and chocolate cubes and cheese cracker cubes and peanut cubes and apricot cereal cubes. And they weren't always easy to manage.

Haise radioed a new, pressing problem down to Vance Brand. "With all these other procedures you've been working on there, I thought I was going to have a new one for you: how to get four gingerbread cubes apart. I think they were stuck together with epoxy."

Brand told him the nutrition experts had to make them tough to withstand the G forces at launch.

"You can tell we're feeling pretty good, Vance, when we start complaining about the food," Haise joked.

But in fact, Haise was starting to feel miserable. His last session in the command module had left him chilled to the bone. His headache had gotten worse, and he felt a fever coming on.

More importantly, something was pushing his spacecraft off course. Haise had noticed something new venting outside the window of the command module. No one could figure out what it was, but it seemed to be affecting their path through space. If they couldn't correct it, and correct it precisely, they were in big trouble.

At about 11:55 a.m. on Friday, April 17, Apollo 13 would come rocketing into Earth's atmosphere at 24,600 miles per hour. That's where the final test would take place—just 60 miles above the Pacific Ocean, where the vacuum of space meets the thick layer of gases that envelops the Earth. And that is when their course would have

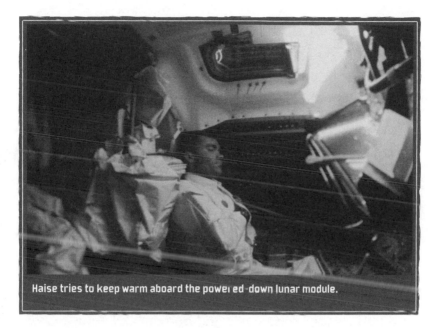
Haise tries to keep warm aboard the powered-down lunar module.

to be exactly on target. Come in a little too shallow and the atmosphere would bounce you right back into space. Come in too steep and you'd plunge so abruptly into the atmosphere that friction would melt the heat shield. The command module would be fried by heat more than three times the temperature of an erupting volcano.

By evening, that was the problem on Jim Lovell's mind. Their course was leaning toward the shallow side of the reentry corridor—the side that would bring them 60 miles from home only to send them hurtling back into space. At 10:30 p.m. Houston time, they were going to fire the thrusters for 15 seconds, just enough to nudge the spacecraft back on course.

Houston had finally given Lovell a way to align the spacecraft for the burn. But he couldn't quite believe what they wanted him to do. At that point, the Earth was only partially lit by the sun. From their perspective it looked just the way the moon does in the early part of its cycle—like a crescent. Houston wanted him to maneuver the spacecraft until one of the crosshairs in his telescope lay neatly across the two points of the crescent—the horns, so to speak. They insisted that would put the ship in exactly the right alignment for the burn.

Lovell wasn't so sure. He and Borman and Anders had tested the Earth alignment on Apollo 8 and decided it was too risky to use as anything but a last resort. You might as well rely on prayer to align a spacecraft, Lovell had thought.

Now, a year and a half later, he had no other choice.

A little after 10 p.m., Haise let Jack Lousma know they were working on the crazy scheme.

"We're manuevering around here to fish for the Earth," he said.

Lovell worked the hand controls for 15 minutes until the blue-and-white crescent appeared exactly where Houston wanted it. At least he was learning how to steer his truck with the 60,000-pound trailer attached.

"Okay, Houston," he reported. "We have our attitude set."

"Roger, Jim," said Jack Lousma.

"I hope the guys in the back room who thought this up knew what they were saying," Lovell added.

Lousma did not respond.

Ten minutes later, the crew took their places. This time, with the equipment powered down, they had no automatic pilot to run the burn for them. They'd have to do it the old-fashioned way. Haise and Lovell gripped the hand controls. Swigert stood by to time the burn on his watch. He watched the second hand sweep around and started the countdown, "Ten . . . nine . . . eight . . ." At "one," Lovell hit a big red button and the LEM engine once again rumbled to life beneath them, this time at a gentle 10 percent of its full power. Haise worked the thrusters to keep the crosshairs of the telescope resting on the horns of the Earth. Swigert called out the seconds as they passed.

When Lovell heard "fourteen," he waited a beat and brought his hand down hard on the shutdown button. As the vibrations of the engine died away, Haise sighted through the telescope. The Earth was exactly where it was supposed to be.

"Okay," said Lousma. "Looks good. Nice work."

"Let's hope it was," said Haise.

———◆———

For Lovell, Haise, and Swigert, the burn meant one more hurdle cleared. In 30 hours they would try to nurse the command module back to life. At that point, they would find out if all the effort of the last three days had been successful. Until then, the mission of the Apollo 13 crew would be a grueling contest of endurance.

Temperatures in the command module had dropped to about 40 degrees. Condensation coated the windows with droplets of water. A tank full of drinking water had frozen solid. When Lovell touched metal in the frigid ship it felt like it sapped the heat from his body and sent it out into space. When he pulled a few hot dogs out of the food locker they had to be thawed before the crew could eat them.

"Okay," said Swigert at one point, "going back up into the refrigerator now."

"Hey, I thought it was the bedroom," said Vance Brand.

"Well, it's got a new name now because it is about 30 degrees cooler."

"Roger," said Brand, "returning to the deep freeze."

By Thursday, Lovell, Haise, and Swigert had given up trying to sleep in *Odyssey*. Haise found a pocket of warmth in the tunnel with his feet stretched back toward the command module. From the LEM it looked like he was sleeping upside down.

In reality, he wasn't sleeping much at all. Haise had developed some kind of infection that gave him a raging fever. He spent a lot of time shivering in a corner of the LEM with his arms clutched to his chest for warmth. At one point, Lovell wrapped Haise in his arms to keep him warm.

As Thursday wore on, Lovell became more and more aware of the ticking clock. John Aaron had been down in Houston for days figuring out how to get the command module powered up. Lovell knew it was a complicated process. Aaron came up with the steps. Ken Mattingly, who still hadn't come down with the measles, tested them out in the simulator. Aaron watched the results and revised the plan. Then they'd go through it all again.

At some point, though, they were going to have to stop. At noon, Lovell told Joe Kerwin, the CAPCOM on duty, that he was eager to have the procedures in hand.

"They exist," Kerwin said, trying to be reassuring. In fact, with about 18 hours to go, Aaron was still revising and re-revising.

And so they waited, sandwiched into a cockpit no bigger than a station wagon. Once or twice, when Kerwin was at the console, he slipped in a bit of news from home. "Everything's running real smooth over in Timber Cove, Jim," he would say. Just a few comforting words—no more than that.

In the afternoon, Haise was moving stuff around to get it stowed for reentry when he came across a small bag with a few personal items he'd been allowed to bring aboard. In it were pictures of his family and a note his pregnant wife had slipped in: "By the time you read this you will already have landed on the moon and, hopefully, be on your way back to Earth. This is to let you know how much we love you, how proud we are of you, and how very much we miss you. Hurry home! Love, Mary."

The message was a sharp reminder of just how far from home they were. Lovell knew he might never make it back to Timber Cove. Haise knew his newest child might be raised without a dad. But they didn't let those thoughts linger, and they didn't talk about them. In the three days since the accident, Lovell, Haise, and Swigert had barely been two feet away from one another. And yet they hadn't shared much about their lives. They hadn't discussed regrets about their pasts or promised to live differently in the future if they made it home.

On a visit to NASA, Mary Haise gets a briefing on the plans to bring her husband home.

Like the engineers in Houston, they were trained to work the problem. Solve one and get ready for the next. For Lovell, getting home was a game of solitaire: Turn over a card and find a place to put it. If you find a place, move on to the next card. Get all the way through the deck, and you make it home. Of course, he might find himself stuck with a card that had nowhere to go. But if that thought was not going to help him win the game, it wasn't worth thinking. It was as simple as that.

As the sun began to set in Houston, Lovell still had plenty of cards to work through—and he'd begun to worry that his crew was in no condition to play them. To conserve supplies, they'd been drinking a meager ration of 6 ounces of water a day. Dehydration had slowed their reaction time. Exhaustion wasn't helping either. In three-and-a-half days, he and Swigert had gotten 12 hours of broken sleep. Haise had logged a few more hours, but he looked worse than his crewmates. His fever had spiked, and shivers rolled through his body in waves.

Somehow, just 10 hours from now, they had to make a course correction, power up a dead command module, jettison a service module and a LEM, and steer their way into Earth's atmosphere. It wasn't simply a matter of pushing a button or two. To get *Odyssey* powered up they would have to throw dozens of switches in exactly the right order. Before they could even start, Houston had to read up the procedures line by line so they could copy them down. That process alone was going to take hours.

All of which left Jim Lovell wondering: What in the heck was Houston doing down there?

CHAPTER 13

DAMAGE DONE

I n Houston, Vance Brand was in the CAPCOM's seat, and it was not a comfortable place to be. It was 6:30 on Thursday night. The control room had been filling with people from the back rooms, eager to hear the plans they'd been working on for days read up to the crew. Lovell, Swigert, and Haise were just as eager to receive them.

Finally, John Aaron walked into the room with a heavy stack of papers in his hands, flanked by Gene Kranz. Until a few minutes ago, Ken Mattingly had been in the simulator testing out the last of the procedures. Aaron still couldn't say they were perfect—for that he needed weeks, not days. But he knew he was out of time.

Aaron deposited a copy of the plans on the CAPCOM's console and Brand told the crew they were ready to go.

"Okay, Vance, I'm ready to copy," said Swigert.

But before they could get started, Kranz and Sy Liebergot called for copies of the plan.

"Okay, Jack, wait one," Brand said. "We want to get one into the hands of FLIGHT and EECOM, and it'll take about a minute or two."

He got no response.

Brand filled the dead air with questions about their water supply. Swigert answered, sounding exhausted.

By the time Kranz and Liebergot had their copies, Brand got word that more controllers were on their way from the back rooms. Each of them needed copies of the plan so they could follow the read through.

"Okay, Jack," Brand cut in again. "All the hordes of people that devised this procedure are going to be coming into the room in a minute, and they'd like to hold up until everybody can listen in."

Someone ran off to make copies of the plan, and Brand was left to stall again.

A half hour later, the copies still hadn't arrived, and everyone on the air-ground loop got a taste of the tension building in the spacecraft.

"Houston, Aquarius." It was Lovell's exasperated voice coming through the loop.

"Go ahead, Aquarius," said Brand.

Lovell launched in: "Vance, we've got to realize that

Vance Brand (center) at the CAPCOM console gets help from Jack Lousma (leaning), Ken Mattingly (standing), and others.

we've got to establish a work-rest cycle up here, so we just can't wait around here to just read procedures all the time up to the burn. We've got to get them up here, look at them, and then we've got to get the people to sleep."

No voices had been raised, no words spoken that couldn't be printed. But the message had been sent. It was Lovell making sure that the engineers understood the urgency of the situation, even with their feet planted firmly on the Earth.

"I know Jim," Brand said. "We're very conscious of

that. We should be ready to go in about 5 minutes. That's all I can say. Stand by."

<hr>

At 11 p.m., in the cramped quarters of the LEM, the plans finally sat in the hands of the crew. Swigert and Haise had scrawled the procedures on pages ripped out of check-lists they no longer needed. It had taken three hours to get through it all—three hours of listening, writing, reading back, and correcting, with sleep-deprived brains and frozen hands.

The crew settled in and tried to sleep, but by 2 a.m. Houston had last-minute revisions to the procedures. Jack Lousma, who had taken over as CAPCOM, urged them to get more rest, but he might as well have been asking them to sleep in a snowbank.

"Well—we'll take it easy," said Swigert, stumbling on his words, "but I—and we'll try to sleep, but it's just awful cold."

There was no rest in sight. They were 70,000 miles from Earth and closing at more than 5,000 miles per hour. In the next ten hours, the pull of gravity would bring them up to five times that speed. There were more revisions to scratch into the checklist. Lovell had to align for one final

Swigert goes over a checklist with Lovell, while the commander tries to keep his hands warm.

burn, just to make sure they didn't come in at too shallow an angle.

In the midst of all the activity, they got a piece of welcome news from Houston: They had enough resources left in the LEM to go ahead and power it up. Until they climbed into *Odyssey* an hour and a half before splashdown, they would ride in style.

"Hey, it's warmed up here now," reported Swigert at around 5 a.m on Friday. "It's almost comfortable."

Lovell had been keeping track of the Earth as they hurtled along, and it was noticeably closer.

"I'm looking out the window now, Jack, and the Earth is whistling in like a high-speed freight train." He jokingly told Lousma that he was still trying to find Fra Mauro, their scheduled landing site on the moon.

"You're going the wrong way, son," Lousma replied.

——◆——

By 7 a.m., the Earth was just five hours away and large enough that it nearly filled the window of the LEM. It had been three and a half days since some kind of explosion rocked the spacecraft, sent their oxygen supply streaming off into space, and ruined their trip to the moon. But they still had no idea what had happened. They'd been dragging the stricken service module for more than 80 hours without any way to see the damage. Now it was time to send the patient into space and get a look at the wound.

Swigert took his place in the still-frigid command module, with Lovell and Haise in the LEM. Two switches stood out from the rest on the panel in front of Swigert. The one on the right fired the exploding bolts to separate the service module from the command module. The one on the left would send the LEM hurtling into space—with Lovell and Haise inside. For hours, Swigert had been worried he would hit the wrong one.

They'd been joking around about just this kind of mistake on Thursday afternoon. Deke Slayton, head of flight crew operations at NASA, had been in the control room laughing about how a bunch of exhausted astronauts could screw up when they jettisoned the LEM.

"Deke says don't forget to close the command module hatch on your way in," radioed the CAPCOM.

"I'm already scared that Jack will have it closed before I get up there," Lovell said.

Everyone got a good laugh out of that, but the whole thing made Swigert sweat. What would happen if his hand slipped at the last minute and jettisoned the LEM instead of the service module? Lovell and Haise would drift away for a second, but with the tunnel open. Just as they realized what had happened, three astronauts would be sucked into the vacuum of space, 40,000 miles from home.

Swigert had dug out a piece of paper and some duct tape and plastered a little sign over the switch labeled "LEM JETT." The sign said in big capital letters, "NO."

At 7:15 a.m., Lovell fired the LEM's thrusters to push the spacecraft forward in the direction of the service

165

module. Swigert hit his switch, and the ship shuddered with a distant *pop*. Lovell reversed the thrusters to pull *Odyssey* and *Aquarius* back.

"SM SEP," he announced in the voice loop as the service module separated from the rest of the ship.

"Copy that," said Joe Kerwin, who was back in the CAPCOM's seat for the final stretch.

For two and half minutes, all three astronauts pressed their faces to the windows, trying to catch a glimpse of the damaged service module.

Damaged: The service module drifts into view with one entire panel blown off the side.

Finally Lovell blurted out, "Okay, I've got her, Houston . . . And there's one *whole* side of that spacecraft missin'."

"Is that right?" Kerwin said, picking up on Lovell's astonishment.

If there had been any lingering doubt about the decision to scrap the moon landing, it was gone now.

"Right by the high gain antenna, the whole panel is blown out, almost from the base to the engine," Lovell said.

"Man, that's unbelievable!" said Haise.

"And Joe," said Lovell, "looks like a lot of debris is just hanging out the side near the S-band antenna."

One-sixth of the service module's shell—a panel measuring about 13 feet by 6 feet—had simply vanished, and the guts of the spacecraft were dangling in space. Lovell couldn't see the oxygen tanks, but a confusing tangle of jagged metal and shiny insulation occupied the shelf where they were supposed to be.

"It's really a mess," said Haise—a mess that could only have been made by a powerful explosion. And given where the damage was on the service module, that explosion happened far too close to the heat shield for comfort.

With four and a half hours to reentry and no way to fix a broken heat shield, Haise decided to keep that thought to himself.

CHAPTER 14

BLACKOUT

As Apollo 13 picked up speed, rocketing toward Earth, one-third of the planet's inhabitants prepared to catch the last installment of the four-day drama on TV or in the newspapers. More than 1 billion people had supposedly followed the crew through their improvised burns and their frigid ordeal. All the major TV networks had been on the air for the milestones of the flight: *"We interrupt our regularly scheduled programming for a special update . . ."* Newspapers had devoted their front pages to the three imperiled astronauts since Wednesday morning. The giant headline in the *Chicago Tribune* this morning read simply: "WORLD AWAITS 3."

The pope offered a prayer for the astronauts at the Vatican in Rome. Sports stadiums went silent to honor the crew. Twelve countries offered to help rescue the spacecraft if it splashed down off target. One of them was the Soviet Union, which buried any hard feelings it had over the space race. The country's leaders ordered two ships to change course and head for the splashdown site. Their astronauts sent a public letter out to their former rivals: "We . . . follow your flight with great attention and concern, and wholeheartedly wish you a safe return to the native earth."

Walter Cronkite summed it up when he declared on a CBS broadcast, "It's not likely that any three men have ever waged such a dramatic battle so fully in the attention of the world."

Nowhere was that attention more focused than in Timber Cove. On the morning of April 17, forty people jammed themselves into the Lovell family room to watch the splashdown. Jeffrey roamed the house in his sailor suit, playing with a little model airplane. Susan had calmed down by now, but nerves in the room were definitely on edge.

For much of the week, Barbara had avoided the family room, but this morning she made her way in. She realized she'd worn a minidress that her father hated. He was gone so much, she sometimes felt like he was surprised to find her grown up. She'd leave for the pool in the bathing suit she wore all the time. He'd look up from the newspaper and say, "Where are you going in that?!" Or she'd leave the house in a miniskirt, and he couldn't resist growling, "You're going to freeze your tail off."

Now she would give anything to hear that voice at home again.

At 9:30 a.m. Jim Lovell's voice reached the Earth from 24,000 miles above the clouds, and it sounded more relaxed than it had since Tuesday night. The crew had finally gotten the go-ahead to power up the command module, a mere two and a half hours before they would use it to blast their way into Earth's atmosphere. Swigert and Haise were up there shivering in the cold while they brought the ship to life.

"We have command module AOS," announced Joe Kerwin, telling Lovell they had acquired a signal from *Odyssey* for the first time since 10:30 on Tuesday night. "Request OMNI Charlie in the CM."

Lovell turned and told his crewmates which antenna Kerwin wanted them to use.

"That," he announced, "was sent through a new onboard communication system known as yelling through the tunnel."

Five minutes later, Kerwin's voice came through again.

Barbara, center, and her family take a break from the crowd in the living room to watch with Barbara's grandmother in the den.

"Just to inform you we've got data from Odyssey, and it looks good."

It was some of the best news Lovell had gotten in four days, and for the moment, it was enough to make him ditch the formal language of the air-ground loop. He had a working ship that just might get him home from the longest ordeal of his life, and "roger" or "affirm" were not the first words that came to mind.

"Hey, great!" was his reply.

Swigert and Haise raced through the checklist to get

Odyssey fully powered up—all 39 pages and 400 steps. The surgeon on duty in Houston noted their heart rates had risen well above resting levels. Down in the LEM, the Earth had taken over Lovell's triangular window and was racing up at him at 11,000 miles an hour.

"Jack, how you coming up there?" he yelled. "The Earth is getting bigger."

Finally, the answer came back that the command module was fully up and running. Lovell wrestled one last time with the hand controls and positioned the ship to jettison the LEM.

"Okay, Houston, Aquarius. I am at the LEM SEP attitude and I'm planning on bailing out," he reported.

"Okay," said Kerwin. "I can't think of a better idea."

Before he drifted through the tunnel, Lovell took a look back at the ship that had kept them alive since the accident. It looked like a zero G garbage dump, paper and other debris floating through the air. Waving aside the trash, he found a souvenir to bring back to Earth. He said good-bye to the lunar lander and floated into the command module. Under his arm was the helmet he would have worn had he been able to walk on the moon.

Twenty-five minutes later, Jack Swigert tore his "NO" warning off the panel and flipped the switch to jettison

Farewell, *Aquarius*: The LEM, with the round tunnel opening in the foreground, drifts away from the command module after separation.

the LEM. Twelve bolts exploded just above their heads with a loud *pop*, and their lifeboat drifted off into space.

"LEM JETT," Lovell reported.

"Okay, copy that," said Kerwin. "Farewell, Aquarius, and we thank you."

———◆———

On Earth, news stations began to broadcast live from the aircraft carrier *Iwo Jima*, stationed 600 miles south of Samoa, where the command module was supposed to splash down. Cameras panned across navy men in their crisp white uniforms, peering into the sky or out into the empty waters of the Pacific. Helicopters patrolled the sky, hoping for a glimpse of the capsule.

The scene played on TV sets around the world. In New York City's Grand Central Terminal, a thousand people stood elbow to elbow, necks craned toward a screen above the ticket windows. In Chicago, more than 400 people gathered in the Admiral television showroom on Michigan Avenue. Hundreds more watched from outside. Nine minutes before splashdown, an ambulance screeched down the street and no one turned to look.

At Timber Cove, Barbara found a place in front of the TV next to her mother and Susan. Jeffrey settled into his mom's lap. All they could do was watch and wait.

———◆———

In Houston, dozens of bleary-eyed engineers streamed into the control room, their work finally done. Kranz's White Team was back on duty, but all the teams were there, milling around the consoles and the outskirts of the room. The VIP gallery above them was packed.

At 11:54 a.m. Houston time, the spacecraft they had worked so hard to bring home would enter the upper reaches of Earth's atmosphere. Friction would build as the command module carved into the thick layer of gases. It was a force powerful enough to slow the ship from 25,000 to 1,000 miles per hour in a matter of minutes, powerful enough to engulf the command module in a 5,000-degree fireball, and powerful enough to cut off all communications with the ground for 3 minutes 38 seconds.

For three-and-a-half days, Mission Control had been a hive of activity. For 3 minutes 38 seconds, it would be forced to grind to a halt. Every ship that came home from space went through the same blackout zone. The engineers with their calculators and their slide rules knew exactly

Thousands gather in New York's Grand Central Terminal, hoping to see a successful splashdown.

how long the blackout would last. If the clock ticked past that mark, and they once again heard Jim Lovell's voice, they would know they had brought the crew home alive. If they heard nothing, it would mean that three astronauts had burned to death 60 miles from home.

———◆———

In the command module, 5,000 miles above the clouds, there wasn't much left to do. Lovell, Haise, and Swigert belted into their seats.

Swigert put himself on the voice loop and said, "I know all of us here want to thank all you guys down there for the very fine job you did."

"That's affirm, Joe," Lovell said.

"I'll tell you we all had a good time doing it," said Kerwin.

The ship was picking up speed fast now, closing in on the 400,000-foot mark, where they would hit the outer reaches of the atmosphere.

"Okay, at 10 minutes to 400K, you're looking good," said Kerwin. "We're real happy with the trajectory, and a minute ago, we just lost contact with your friend Aquarius."

"She sure was a good ship," said Swigert, his voice breaking a little.

On the ground, Kranz was doing his final checks with the controllers:

"EECOM, you go?"

"Go, Flight," said John Aaron.

"RETRO?"

"Go."

"Guidance?"

"Go."

With three minutes left, there were no objections.

"Okay," Kerwin reported. "We just had one last time around the room and everybody says you're looking great . . . Welcome home."

"Thank you," said Swigert.

A minute later, a pink glow replaced the blackness of space around the ship. Lovell, Haise, and Swigert felt the force of gravity at their backs for the first time in six days. Pink changed to violet, then bright orange and red. G forces built beyond anything they had felt at launch, like a giant hand pressing down on their chests. A display signaled that the ship had dropped below orbital speed: They would not be bouncing back into space. Earth's gravity had captured them for good. And yet, the voices at Mission Control that had kept them company for six days were gone, replaced by a whining static. They might as well have been on the far side of the moon.

Standing at the flight director's console, surrounded by controllers, Gene Kranz felt intensely lonely. No one spoke. There was only the hum of the consoles and the air-conditioning, the occasional zip of a lighter firing up a cigarette, the empty static in the headsets connecting the men in the room to the astronauts.

All eyes were fixed on the digital clock at the front of the room as it counted down the seconds until those headsets should spring back to life: 03:38 . . . 03:37 . . . 03:36 . . . While they waited, Kranz lost himself in his own thoughts. He was trained not to dwell in the past. Yet he couldn't help combing through all the decisions he'd made in the last four days, hoping they'd been the right ones. All the while, the clock kept ticking: 01:22 . . . 01:21 . . . 01:20 . . .

Directly below Kranz, John Aaron was feeling good about what they'd accomplished: keeping three men alive on the resources of the LEM, powering up a cold command module and doing it with just two hours' worth of power. One of the giant monitors at the front of the room now carried the view from the *Iwo Jima*. Aaron fully expected to see the command module in the sky in a few minutes, floating to the ocean under three billowing parachutes.

When the clock on the wall hit zero, Kranz told Kerwin to radio the ship.

"Odyssey, Houston, standing by," Kerwin said into the voice loop.

No response.

Fifteen seconds later, Kerwin tried again.

Still no response.

The digital clock churned in the other direction now, counting the seconds since they should have heard Lovell or Swigert or Haise hailing them from the ship: 00:42 . . . 00:43 . . . 00:44.

Like everyone else in the room, John Aaron felt his heart sink. Lovell's description of the service module flashed in his mind—an entire panel gone, a tangled mess of metal and insulation. The explosion must have ruined the heat shield. Was this really all there was to it? They had worked the problem around the clock for nearly four days and they were going to lose three astronauts this close to home?

Then, nearly a minute and a half after the clock had reached zero, a voice crackled through a speaker, straight from the *Iwo Jima*.

"ARIA 4 has acquisition."

A C-135 jet, scanning the skies for Apollo 13, had picked up a signal.

Splashdown: The command module makes a soft landing in the Pacific Ocean, less than a mile from its target.

Flight directors Gerald Griffin (giving the thumbs-up), Gene Kranz, and Glynn Lunney lead the cheers at splashdown.

Kranz pounded his fist on his console. John Aaron could feel tears welling up in his eyes.

"Odyssey, Houston, standing by," repeated Kerwin.

"Okay, Joe," came Swigert's reply.

"Okay, we read you, Jack."

Three minutes later, the screen at mission control flashed the best sight anyone could remember seeing: a tiny capsule suspended from its three red-and-white main parachutes, floating gently toward the ocean.

The entire room erupted in applause. Kranz felt himself begin to cry. He tried to choke it back, but the effort made it worse. He gave in and stood at his flight director's console, tears streaming down his face.

Kerwin switched on his mike and tried to talk over the cheers.

"Odyssey, Houston, we show you on the mains; it really looks great!"

———◆———

The image went out instantly across the globe—the command module bringing Lovell, Haise, and Swigert safely to rest in the Pacific Ocean. At Grand Central Terminal, the wall-to-wall crowd burst into applause.

Outside the TV showroom in Chicago, a woman shouted: "There it is! It's terrific."

At the American embassy in London, the telephone operator was deluged with calls. "People were sobbing with obvious relief and happiness," she told a reporter. "I just don't know what to say to them."

———◆———

In Timber Cove, the champagne corks started popping. Astronauts Pete Conrad, Neil Armstrong, and Buzz Aldrin were the first ones at the refrigerator. Like Jim Lovell, they had each left the planet and come home again. Each of them knew what it was like to feel the Earth safe under your feet for the first time in days.

For Barbara and her mother, relief hadn't come until the very last second, when the blunt end of the capsule settled into the ocean. As they sat through the blackout, Barbara's mom had been squeezing Jeffrey tighter and tighter. Finally, when the ship hit the water, he cried out—not in celebration but in pain.

As drinks were poured and tears flowed, a friend came up to Barbara's mother and told her there was a phone call for her. President Nixon was on the line. Her mother disappeared into the bedroom to take the call. When she came out, she announced that she had plans for tomorrow. She'd be flying to Hawaii aboard Air Force One to greet the astronauts when they arrived. Barbara was crushed to find there was no room for the kids, but not because she wanted to ride on the presidential plane. She could care less about that. She just wanted to see her dad.

⎯⎯⎯◈⎯⎯⎯

Two days later, Barbara stood at Ellington Field air force base in Houston with the Haise kids. Behind them a crowd of nearly 2,000 people had gathered to welcome the Apollo 13 crew home. At 9 p.m., a backup presidential plane touched down with Barbara's father inside. He probably wouldn't be home for long. There'd be some kind of tour. He'd be out giving press conferences and meeting world leaders and riding in parades. After that, maybe he'd be done with flying. Maybe he'd be home more often.

Then again, maybe he wouldn't. But right now, Barbara didn't care. Her dad would get off the plane, and she would get to hug him. She and the Haise kids looked up at a full moon, big and round in the night sky, and all she could think was how good it felt that her father was down here and not up there. For now, that was all that mattered.

Celebration: Marilyn Lovell, with Jeffrey in her lap, watches her husband land in the Pacific.

SPACESHIP EARTH

O ne of the most beautiful sights we saw was the sight of the Earth getting bigger as we came back," Swigert said when the crew set foot on solid ground for the first time in a week.

The three astronauts were relieved to be safe on Earth. But now that they weren't fighting for their lives, disappointment crept in. Lovell confronted the fact that he would probably never return to space. He'd flown four missions, and it was time for him to step aside. Haise and Swigert, the rookies, might still fly again. But for now, they felt like they had failed.

"We didn't get it done," said Haise.

It had been a grueling trip back. Lovell had lost 14 pounds during the 6-day flight. Haise had developed a kidney infection from dehydration and had to be

Coming Home: Haise, Lovell, and Swigert greet the crew of the *Iwo Jima* after landing in the Pacific.

pumped full of antibiotics. You would think they had earned a vacation.

Instead, they said a quick hello to their families on Sunday night and reported to NASA first thing Monday morning to answer endless questions about the flight. It was time to figure out what had gone wrong.

It would take NASA two months to make their final report. They traced the problem to one tiny thermostat in the oxygen tanks. The thermostat was supposed to operate like the temperature controls in a house. When the tanks were heated, it automatically kept the temperature from rising above 80 degrees Fahrenheit. This little device somehow made it into the Apollo program with a serious design flaw. The launch operation at Cape Kennedy ran on a 65-volt electrical system, but the thermostat could only handle 28 volts.

Under normal circumstances, that wouldn't have been a problem. The thermostat had almost nothing to do. Temperatures in the oxygen tanks weren't supposed to rise above negative 100 degrees Fahrenheit, much less get up to 80. But one of the tanks that would eventually be loaded onto Apollo 13 had a small defect. It had been dropped about 2 inches by technicians in 1968. NASA tested it and decided it hadn't been damaged. But a month before Lovell, Haise, and Swigert took off for the moon, a ground crew tried to empty the tank after a routine test. When it wouldn't empty properly they heated the liquid oxygen to boil it into a gas and force it through the lines. As the heat in the tank rose, it triggered the thermostat. The little device with the fatal flaw got a jolt of 65 volts and melted shut. The temperature inside the tanks shot up to 1,000 degrees, scorching the insulation on some wiring in the tank. No one knew it had happened because the gauges monitoring the tanks only went up to 80 degrees.

Meet the Press. Jeffrey clings to Barbara while the family answers questions from the mob of reporters that had been waiting on Lazywood Lane for four days.

So when Lovell, Haise, and Swigert lifted off on April 11, 1970, they were carrying a time bomb in their service module. Fifty-five hours later, Swigert flipped a switch to stir the oxygen tanks. Electric current surged through the damaged wires, and the insulation started smoldering. Pure oxygen can turn a flicker into a raging fire in a matter of seconds, and that's exactly what happened. Gas exploded out of tank 2. The blast damaged tank 1, blew a panel off the service module, and turned a mission to the moon into a battle for survival. All because of a single tiny thermostat.

During their first days back, Haise braced himself for headlines reading, "NASA WASTES $400 MILLION." Instead, the mission was hailed as a great success. President Nixon met the astronauts in Hawaii and handed each of them the Medal of Freedom—the highest honor an American civilian can receive. They were heroes, Nixon said. They had reminded everyone that "in this age of technicians and scientific marvels . . . the individual still counts." And, the president claimed, Lovell, Haise, and Swigert had helped bring the world together. "Wherever

Swigert and Lovell get a hero's welcome with a ticker tape parade in Chicago. Haise was stuck in Houston recovering from the kidney infection he got during the mission.

people live in this world, wherever they are, they value human life and they thought of these three men not as Americans, but as human beings, courageous men, and they wanted them to be saved. If only we could think in that way about every individual on this earth, we could truly have a world of peace."

It was a nice thought.

But while part of the world was rooting for Lovell, Haise, and Swigert, the rest of it seemed to be falling apart. Eight thousand miles from Houston, in Vietnam, American troops had been fighting an unpopular war for six years. Thirteen days after Nixon spoke about Apollo 13 and world peace, he expanded the Vietnam War. Thousands of American troops crossed the Vietnamese border into Cambodia. Hundreds of thousands of antiwar protesters took to the streets all across the United States. At Kent State University in Ohio, a rally got out of hand. Police opened fire into a crowd of students, and when the shooting stopped, four people were dead and nine wounded.

Two weeks after the triumph of Apollo 13, the rest of America had come back to Earth too. The sight of the command module floating safely into the Pacific Ocean had been replaced by another image that was impossible to forget: a young woman screaming in shock and anger over the dead body of a Kent State student.

Demonstrators call for an end to the Vietnam War, three weeks after police opened fire on a student protest at Kent State University.

For more than a decade, politicians and NASA executives had pointed to the space program as a beacon of success in a murky, frightening world. Every successful launch seemed to prove that smart people armed with the latest technology can achieve miracles. *We made it to the moon!* So if we put our minds to it, couldn't we solve any problem in the universe? After Lovell's first flight around the moon in 1968, the head of NASA, Thomas Paine, said he hoped it would serve as a lesson to "restless students" everywhere:

Give up drugs in favor of calculators and computers, and you could accomplish anything.

But flying to the moon had cost the country billions of dollars, while there were problems right here on Earth that weren't getting solved. After Apollo 8, the *New York Times* sent a reporter to Detroit, where jobs were scarce and the poverty rate high. The reporter found that African Americans were especially unimpressed by the space program. At the time, there wasn't a single person of color in the astronaut corps or on the floor at Mission Control. And people wondered why NASA had so much money when their neighbors were struggling to put a roof over their heads. "Before one more dollar is spent on outer space," demanded civil rights activist Charles Evers, "we must make sure that not one child here on Earth goes to a dinner table with no food on it."

By the time Lovell, Haise, and Swigert returned to Earth, flying to the moon had lost a lot of its appeal. NASA had planned to fly seven more missions after Apollo 13. Instead, they shut the program down after Apollo 17. Neither Swigert nor Haise made it back to the moon. The space shuttle followed Apollo, and for three decades it ferried astronauts to and from the International Space Station orbiting Earth. But no human being has left Earth orbit since December 1972.

That's enough to make you wonder—what was the point? In 1964, when Lovell was training as an astronaut, *Life* magazine predicted that a walk on the moon would be just the beginning. Before long we'd have nuclear-powered ferries shuttling people to a permanent base on the lunar surface. We'd build space stations where "men bound for the planets" could resupply and refuel. Fred Haise thought the space program might be a way to "establish the human race elsewhere."

Instead, six moon landings brought back 850 pounds of moon rocks and soil. None of it told us much about the origin of the moon or life on Earth. And none of it brought us closer to colonizing another planet.

But flying to the moon may have brought us closer to the Earth. Between 1968 and 1972, 24 astronauts flew into lunar orbit and back, and many of them had some kind of life-changing revelation along the way. Edgar Mitchell, who spent nine hours on the moon during Apollo 14, said the biggest joy came on the way back home. As the spacecraft spun through the sky, he saw Earth, the moon, the sun, and countless stars—"a whole 360-degree panorama of the heavens." He knew from studying physics that the molecules that make up people and mountains and everything on Earth had their origin in the stars billions of years ago. Now he felt it in his bones. "It was an overwhelming sense of oneness, of connectedness," he said. "It wasn't them and us. It was, 'That's me; that's all one thing.'"

Alan Bean, the lunar module pilot on Apollo 12, came back with a new love for the planet he had left behind for ten days. "Since that time, I've not complained about weather one single time; I'm glad there is weather. I've not complained about traffic. I'm glad there's people around . . . Why do people complain about the Earth? We are living in the garden of Eden."

In April 1970, six months after Bean's mission and five days after Lovell, Haise, and Swigert came back from space, 20 million people participated in the first annual Earth Day. Groups wielding shovels, rakes, and bags cleaned up trash in parks and along highways. Crowds gathered in Washington, D.C., and in state capitals, demanding new laws to control pollution. Students in 10,000 schools sat in special classes to learn about threats to the environment. It was the beginning of the modern environmental movement—a coordinated attempt to save Earth from the people who live on it.

Thanks to the Apollo program, the people who planned Earth Day saw the planet a little differently than every generation before them. They remembered the "Earthrise" photo that Lovell, Borman, and Anders sent back from their first journey to the moon. "Not until Apollo 8 sent back Earth's self-portrait were millions able to see and realize how 'small and blue and beautiful' this planet is," wrote the editors of the *New York Times* three days before the first Earth Day. When poet Archibald MacLeish saw that photo, he described the Earth as a "tiny raft in an enormous, empty night." Lovell, who saw that tiny raft in person, thought it looked like an "oasis in the vast blackness of space." When you stand on the Earth the planet feels like a given; you take it for granted. When you see it hanging in space with all the other lifeless stars and planets, it looks lush and vibrant—and fragile as an egg.

Flying to the moon didn't exactly transform our behavior on Earth. Factories, cars, and other sources now pump twice the volume of greenhouse gases into the air as they did in 1970. But maybe—just maybe—the view from space made us more aware of the consequences.

As Fred Haise once put it, "We think we live on a big object called the Earth, but it's really a very small object. It's a single spacecraft. We don't have a backup for Earth."

GLOSSARY

asteroid: a space rock, much smaller than a planet, that orbits the sun

atmosphere: a layer of gases surrounding the Earth or another planet

circuit breaker: a switch that interrupts the flow of electricity in a system of wires and equipment

console: a panel with controls or monitors for electronic or mechanical equipment

epoxy: a type of high-strength glue

fuel cell: a device that produces electricity when two or more chemicals are combined

instrumentation: devices such as gauges used for measuring or control

jettison: to get rid of something, usually from an aircraft or ship

lunar: having to do with the moon

orbit: a curved path around a planet, star, or other body in space

satellite: human-made device placed in orbit for observation or communication

simulation: an exercise designed to be just like the real world, usually for the purpose of training someone

splashdown: technique by which a spacecraft lands in a body of water

test pilot: pilot who flies a new aircraft to test its performance in flight

thruster: small rocket engine used to make precise corrections in a spacecraft's path

AUTHOR'S NOTE

As I write this, I already miss working on this book. Historians usually grope their way toward the past through memories recorded decades after the fact. If they're lucky they find diaries or letters written close to the moment. People who write about the space program, however, get to witness what happened in real time. NASA recorded every minute of dialogue between their crews and Mission Control and between the flight directors and their controllers. Those recordings are available to anyone with an internet connection.

This was mostly a great asset. It was also a curse. A book about a mission to the moon does not get written when the author can't stop listening to the astronauts. Search for "Apollo 13 full mission 12," and you'll see what I mean. You can't hear the bang from the explosion, but you can hear Lovell cut the syllables short when he says,

"Houston, we've had a problem." Now search "Apollo 13 flight director's loop." You can feel the penny drop for Gene Kranz when he says, "Crew thinks they are *venting* something." You get anxious for the controllers when they don't answer Glynn Lunney's questions fast enough. I didn't watch the wonderful movie *Apollo 13* while I was writing the book because I didn't want it to influence the way I told the story. But listening to the tapes was just as good.

Even with such vivid sources, I was struck by how hard it is to reconstruct a piece of the past accurately. A lot of the story of Apollo 13 happened "off mike." No one recorded Gene Kranz's speech to the controllers in the back room. There were no microphones in the Lovell house when Barbara learned that her father was in trouble. For those experiences we have only memory, and memory is notoriously unreliable. People tend to recall important experiences in their lives better than they remember going to the grocery store on a random Saturday. But that doesn't mean they remember everything accurately. When I talked to Barbara Lovell, more than 45 years separated our conversations from that week in April 1970. She was convinced at first that she didn't go to school the entire week. Later, I found a newspaper photo of her getting into her car on the second day of the crisis. The caption claimed she was on her way to school. When I showed it to Barbara, she thought the reporters might have just assumed that's what she was doing. But she realized she didn't completely trust her memory.

The emotions, however, were as vivid as ever. She remembers the dreams about her dad dying. She can describe what it was like to be thirteen years old and setting the dinner table after finding out that three astronauts who worked with her father had just burned to death. Even now, she has trouble getting through an entire conversation about Apollo 13 without crying.

The astronauts and the engineers were a little harder to figure out. What they were doing was incredibly dangerous. When Lovell took off to circle the moon in Apollo 8, there were scientists at NASA who felt the crew had a 50-50 chance of coming back. A year and a half later, when Neil Armstrong and Buzz Aldrin walked on the moon, President Nixon had a speech ready in case the LEM failed to lift off the lunar surface. It read: "Fate has ordained that the men who went to the moon to explore in peace will stay on the moon to rest in peace. These brave men, Neil Armstrong and Edwin Aldrin, know that there is no hope for their recovery, but they also know that there is hope for mankind in their sacrifice."

How did the astronauts cope with the danger? It's hard to tell. They were trained to be cool under pressure. And they weren't especially quick to talk about their emotions. When reporters asked Lovell, Haise, and Swigert if they'd been frightened during the flight, they usually said something like, "We had work to do; there wasn't time to be scared." Alan Bean was one of the few astronauts who admitted getting anxious in space. He couldn't help looking out the window and thinking that if it broke he'd be dead in seconds. "There was death right on the other side of the window," he said.

If flying in space brought death so close, why did they do it? Lovell had a typically practical answer to that question. "The rewards involved outweighed the risks involved," he said. In another moment he confessed he was "addicted" to space flight, and maybe that was closer to the truth. Maybe the answer is the same for many astronauts as it is for Everest climbers and BASE jumpers and soldiers who choose to return to war zones when their tour of duty is done. When death is just outside the window, life feels more vivid, more urgent. Frank Borman, who circled the moon with Lovell in Apollo 8, put it this way when his wife tried to get him to stop flying: "There's more to this life than just living."

Many of the people who were part of Apollo 13 had long careers at NASA. They participated in mission after mission. But they remember Apollo 13 as a highlight of their lives. Forty-five years later, John Aaron can still get choked up when he describes the moment the spacecraft appeared on the big monitors at Mission Control, floating safely under its parachutes. For four days, he'd been making decisions that could mean the difference between life and death for three men. That, I suppose, is more than just living.

SOURCES

Books

Baker, David. *Apollo 13: Owners' Workshop Manual.* Minneapolis: Zenith, 2013.

———. *The History of Manned Spaceflight.* New York: Crown, 1982.

Chaikin, Andrew. *Voices from the Moon.* New York: Penguin, 2009.

———. *A Man on the Moon.* New York: Viking Penguin, 1994.

Collins, Michael. *Carrying the Fire.* New York: Farrar, Straus, and Giroux, 1974.

Cooper, Henry S.F. Jr. *XIII: The Apollo Flight That Failed.*
Baltimore: Johns Hopkins Press, 1972.

Dean, Margaret Lazarus. *Leaving Orbit: Notes from the Last
Days of American Spaceflight.* Minneapolis: Graywolf
Press, 2015.

Godwin, Robert, ed. *Apollo 13: The NASA Mission Reports.*
Burlington, Ontario: Apogee Books, 2000.

Kranz, Eugene F. *Failure Is Not an Option.* New York: Simon
& Schuster, 2000.

Lovell, Jim and Jeffrey Kluger. *Lost Moon.* New York:
Houghton Mifflin, 1994.

Murray, Charles and Catherine Bly Cox. *Apollo: The Race
to the Moon.* New York: Simon & Schuster, 1989.

Reynolds, David West. *Apollo: The Epic Journey to the
Moon, 1963–1972.* Minneapolis: Zenith, 2013.

Tribbe, Matthew D. *No Requiem for the Space Age.* New
York: Oxford University Press, 2014.

Wolfe, Tom. *The Right Stuff*. New York: Farrar, Straus & Giroux, 1979.

Oral Histories, Interviews, and Transcripts

Aaron, John. Interview with the author. Dec. 15, 2015.

———. Interview with Kevin M. Rusnak for Johnson Space Center. Houston, Texas, Jan 26, 2000.

Haise, Fred. Interview with Doug Ward for Johnson Space Center. Houston, Texas, March 23, 1999.

Harrison, Barbara Lovell. Interview with the author. Nov. 16, 2015.

Keck, Connie. Interview with the author. Dec. 8, 2015.

Kranz, Eugene F. Interview with Roy Neal for Johnson Space Center. Houston, Texas, April 28, 1999.

Liebergot, Seymour. Interview with Michelle Kelly for Johnson Space Center. Houston, Texas, April 27, 1998.

Loden, Hal. Interview with the author. Feb. 26, 2016.

Lovell, James A. Interview with Ron Stone for Johnson Space Center. Houston, Texas, May 25, 1999.

———. Interview with Robert Sherrod. Houston, Texas, June 28–29, 1974.

———. Fred Haise, Jack Swigert. Apollo 13 Post Flight Press Conference. Houston, Texas, April 21, 1970.

———. Fred Haise, Jack Swigert. "Apollo 13 Technical Crew Debriefing, April 24, 1970," Mission Operations Brance, Flight Crew Support Division, Manned Spacecraft Center. Houston, Texas.

———. Gene Kranz, Jim Mattingly, Fred Haise. "40th Anniversary of Apollo 13: Annual John H. Glenn Lecture." Smithsonian National Air and Space Museum, April 15, 2010.

Lunney, Glynn. "Apollo XIII." Johnson Space Center, NASA. http://www.jsc.nasa.gov/history/oral_histories /LunneyGS/Apollo13.htm

Mattingly, Thomas K. Interview with Rebecca Wright for Johnson Space Center. Costa Mesa, California, Nov. 6, 2001.

NASA. "Apollo 13 Mission Commentary" transcript.

———. "Apollo 13 Technical Air-To-Ground Voice Transcription"

———. "Apollo 13 Timeline"

———. "Report of Apollo 13 Review Board," June 15, 1970.

Documentaries

Apollo 13: The Real Story. Dateline NBC, April 13, 2010.

Apollo 13: To the Edge and Back. Directed by Noel Buckner and Rob Whittlesey. TV movie, July 20, 1994.

Houston, We've Got a Problem. Directed by Don Wiseman. NASA, 1972.

In the Shadow of the Moon. Directed by David Sington. 2007.

The Story of the Sputnik Moment. Directed by David Hoffman. Varied Directions, Inc., 2008.

Newspapers, Magazines, and TV News

Chicago Tribune. Coverage of space program, 1959–1972.

Life magazine. "Their Prodigious Chariot," Dec. 14, 1959.

———. "The Eerie World of Zero G," March 21, 1960.

———. "What Looms Ahead: Space, Part II," Oct. 2, 1964.

———. "How Will Man Suit Up for Space?" April 16, 1965.

———. "Astronauts' Own Reports from Gemini 6 and 7," Jan. 14, 1966.

———. "Ever Nearer to Target Moon," Jan. 26, 1968.

———. "The Fire and Fate Have Left Eight Widows," Jan. 26, 1968.

———. "Christmas Cheers on the Apollo 8 Homefront," Jan. 10, 1969.

———. "Apollo VIII: The Astronauts Write Their Stories of the Flight," Jan. 17, 1969.

———. "The Joyous Triumph of Apollo 13," April 24, 1970.

———. "The Three Astronauts Tell What Happened Aboard the Crippled Apollo 13," May 1, 1970.

The New York Times. Coverage of space program, 1959–1972.

ACKNOWLEDGMENTS

Much of this story has been told in oral histories, books, and documentary films, and I'm grateful to the astronauts and engineers who have shared their memories so many times. John Aaron and Hal Loden were generous enough to do it yet again for me. They also answered technical questions along the way with a patience and attention to detail that hasn't waned since their days in Mission Control.

The children of the astronauts, by contrast, have not often been asked to tell their stories. Barbara Lovell Harrison was kind enough to share hers with me. She dug up often painful memories with care and thoughtfulness—and put up with a pesky stream of email queries for months. Thanks also to Connie Keck, who was Barbara's best friend and rock during the astronaut years and after.

Thanks to Vermont College of Fine Arts, and to Jim Nolte and his staff at the Gary Library there. Thanks also to Bill Barry and Nora Normandy at NASA's Johnson Space Center archives.

I'm grateful to friends and colleagues Elizabeth Ward, Mark Aronson, John Glenn, Leda Schubert, Daphne Kalmar, Jeff Fannon, John Hollar, and Rick VandenBergh; to Paige Hazzan and everyone at Scholastic who make this series possible; to the exceptional Miriam Altshuler; and especially to Laura Williams McCaffrey for the endless pages read and the encouragement offered.

Much more than thanks are due to Estie Lawrence and Richard Olson; and always to Jill, Zoe, and Finn.

ABOUT THE AUTHOR

TOD OLSON is author of the historical fiction series *How to Get Rich* and the first book in this series, *Lost in the Pacific, 1942*. He works as an editor, holds an MFA from Vermont College of Fine Arts, and lives in Vermont with his family, his mountain bike, and his electric reclining chair.